The Marriage of Love

How to Communicate, Build a Strong Relationship, and Improve Intimacy with Your Partner - From Date Nights, Engagement Rings and Wedding Dresses, to Newlyweds and Anniversaries

Juliet Welles

To Walter, forever my Romeo.

Table of Contents

INTRODUCTION 1

CHAPTER 1: COHABITING AND MARRIAGE—PEOPLE'S RELATIONSHIP
PREFERENCES AND CHOICES 3

Let's Look at Some Couple Stats *4*
*Opinions on Cohabitation, Partnerships, and Marriage: What Do Americans
Say?* *8*
Why Do Stats Matter? *9*
*The Biggest Long-Term Relationship Issues Today & 10 Reasons to Keep on
Reading* *10*

CHAPTER 2: BASIC COMMUNICATION 15

THE ART OF LISTENING 16
WHO'S IN WHO'S SHOES? 18
THE IMPACT OF YOUR VOICE 20
BODY LANGUAGE 22
PROACTIVITY VERSUS REACTIVITY 28

CHAPTER 3: THE 5 LOVE LANGUAGES 31

WHO IS DR. GARY CHAPMAN? 32
THE QUIZ YOU NEED TO TAKE 33
The First Love Language: Words of Affirmation *33*
The Second Love Language: Acts of Service *36*
The Third Love Language: Receiving Gifts *40*
The Fourth Love Language: Quality Time *41*
The Fifth Love Language: Physical Touch *43*
THIS IS WHAT YOU SHOULDN'T DO 46

CHAPTER 4: STOP THROWING THINGS! 49

JEALOUSY 50
INSECURITIES 52
PRIDE 56
HORMONES (YES, HORMONES) 58
THOSE CHOICES 61

CHAPTER 5: LESSONS LEARNED 65

    COMMON LESSONS THAT PEOPLE LEARN.....................................66
    WHAT YOUR PARTNER NEEDS TO KNOW ABOUT YOUR PAST 69
    LEARN FROM IT 72

CHAPTER 6: THE (IN)FAMOUS APOLOGY 77

    WHAT APOLOGIZING CAN DO FOR YOUR RELATIONSHIP.............................77
    Good Idea Versus Bad Idea.....................................80
    Don't Apologize for These Things in Your Relationship 82
    REMEMBER THE 5 LOVE LANGUAGES? HERE ARE THE 5 LANGUAGES OF APOLOGY 85
    The Importance of Knowing You and Your Partner's Language of Apology.87
    THE DARK SIDE OF AN APOLOGY 88

CHAPTER 7: WHO WANTS A BABY? 91

    IS THERE A PERFECT TIME? 91
    DO WE BOTH WANT THE SAME THING? 94
    WHERE DO BABIES COME FROM? 96
    POST-BABY GETAWAYS AND DATES 101

CHAPTER 8: THE IMPORTANCE OF SELF-CARE 103

    MENTAL SELF-CARE 104
    PHYSICAL SELF-CARE 107
    COUPLES' SELF CARE 109
    KEEP YOUR SENSE OF STYLE—IT ROCKS! 113
    SHARE YOUR CARE 114

CHAPTER 9: QUIRKY DATE IDEAS 117

CHAPTER 10: DON'T FORGET ABOUT SEX 123

    THE IMPORTANCE OF HEALTHY SEX 124
    ARE MEN REALLY FROM MARS AND WOMEN REALLY FROM VENUS?.............127
    SEXY STRATEGIES 130
    READ THIS IF YOU PLAY WITH TOYS 132

CONCLUSION 135

REFERENCES.....................................139

Introduction

Relationships are as unique as the people in them. Yet, there are components of these bonds that can make them so startlingly similar. When it comes to navigating a partnership or marriage, both the individual and our common human nature are important to consider, and both aspects should be used to form a contextual lens through which the relationship or marriage can be viewed. However, that context can change over time without partners even noticing, which can lead to new wants and needs. If one partner is still using the old lens in a situation like this, possibly because their own wants and needs have not changed as significantly as their partner's, it can cause conflict or dissatisfaction in the relationship. In this sense, context can refer to a partner's wants, needs, as well as surroundings, and because there are so many different things going on in each of our lives at one time, it's quite easy to overlook a subtle change. So, what should be done? How can these changes that cause potential rifts in a relationship or marriage be managed with minimum conflict and dissonance between partners?

Fortunately, there are ways to keep a relationship on track if it's still going strong, and there are also ways to work on a relationship that seems to have taken its final breath—that is, if you are prepared to fight. If it worked at some stage, there should be a reason to fight. The smartest choice you can make in a relationship is to familiarize yourself with different tools that can help you work through conflict, understand your partner, and stay proactive to avoid any unnecessary issues that may develop between the two of you. Many of these tools revolve around effective communication, but there's a lot more one can learn to finetune relationship skills.

This guide will cover all the dusty corners of relationship building that are often overlooked, by digging deeper into the cornerstones of successful relationships.

While we are all different, one thing that brings us together is our ability to love, be loved, and to show dedication and loyalty towards our partners. We are beautiful in this way, and sharing these special gifts with the ones we love most, should be cherished and respected. May you find enlightenment, inspiration, and a few laughs from this guide to a prosperous relationship and marriage.

Chapter 1:

Cohabiting and Marriage—People's

Relationship Preferences and Choices

There are lots of reasons why couples decide to move in together but not get married immediately! Some don't get married at all or live only with an un-officiated partnership. One of the most interesting types of partnerships I've ever come to know about was the famous and eccentric relationship between philosopher Jean-Paul Sartre and his fellow existentialist and celebrated feminist partner Simone de Beauvoir. In the beginning, they based their relationship on a contract that was renewable after two years if they felt they wanted to abandon ship. During their lifelong relationship, the partners didn't live together, and they had an agreement to pursue other love interests. Even though this was what they agreed upon, this non-traditional approach to a long-term partnership caused them a lot of pain and heartache, especially when one of them decided to act on this agreement and form a relationship with a third party. One must keep in mind that these were two highly intelligent individuals who had strong opinions about relationships and gender, especially de Beauvoir. Nevertheless, they loved each other, and when Sartre passed away, de Beauvoir was overcome with grief. In a case like this, where they were so obviously in love with each other, you can't help asking yourself, why did they decide to follow these relationship arrangements? Did they not yearn to make a living together like most couples do? The habits and choices of partners in long-term relationships have been a focus of academic study for quite some time. Even though every couple has their individual wants and needs, there is that general component that is related to human nature as we mentioned earlier. It is these components that are studied to find out why couples make the choices they make. The outcome of these studies leads to some interesting and valuable insight into different relationship choices.

Let's Look at Some Couple Stats

In our time, which is more than half-a-decade later than Sartre and Beauvoir's, it has also become more difficult to do marriage the traditional way. While lots of people still get married, another approach to long-term relationships, namely cohabitation, has also become popular. Sometimes this arrangement will lead to an engagement and subsequent marriage, and sometimes it won't. Before we jump into how to steer a relationship in the right direction and how to save one from ending up on the rocks, let's look at what people's preferences are, how these preferences have changed in the past century, and which factors may play defining roles.

According to recent research conducted in 2019, there are now more partners living together with long-term partnership agreements than there are marriages. Research also indicates that marriages still provide that sense of security for couples as married couples are more trusting of their partners and the level of satisfaction is higher in a relationship consummated by marriage. Cohabitation without marriage is an acceptable practice in American society as it appears that the number of couples who are delaying marriage or deciding not to tie the knot at all is on the rise. This makes cohabitation a rational choice for those who want to stay in a long-term relationship. According to a recent survey, there is still a smaller section of American society who expresses their approval towards couples who eventually decide to get married.

The societal stance on cohabitation and marriage is very much diverse as, according to the same 2019 survey, 69% of individuals say that they have no problem with couples cohabiting even if they have no plans of getting married. Sixteen percent of individuals say that they agree with cohabitation, but only if the couple have plans to get married, and 16%

say that cohabitation without getting married is under no circumstances acceptable. To put society's opinion into context, in 2002, 54% of couples had been in a cohabiting situation, whereas 60% of couples had been married for some time. From 2013-2017, 59% of couples had been in a cohabiting situation while only 50% had ever been married. Most recently, 46% of society thinks that it's fine for couples to stay together even if there are no wedding plans, while 53% feel that it will benefit their relationship if they get married.

One of the reasons that some couples decide to get married and some decide to stay unmarried partners is due to religious beliefs and cultural upbringings. Even then, religious individuals do not necessarily believe that others should marry, even if they do believe this for themselves. Good for them! People should be allowed to make their own choices. Keeping that in mind, there are still some key findings that came out of these studies from the Pew Research Center. Let's look at what the research and surveys, conducted on 5,579 married adults and 880 adults who were, at that time, living with an unmarried partner, including same-sex relationships, had to say:

1. If you are married, you will likely feel more secure in your relationship, have a stronger trust relationship, and have a higher level of relationship satisfaction. This doesn't mean that couples that are satisfied with cohabiting are not able to reach these levels of satisfaction and trust, but when looking at the figures, there is always a 10%-20% difference between aspects like acting in a partner's best interest, the likeliness of being unfaithful, general honesty, and working responsibly with finances. Adding to these interesting outcomes, there is also 10%-15% between the level of satisfaction between cohabiting partners and married couples when it comes to how they view their partner's approach to parenting with children under the age of 18, the way they divide and cooperate when it comes to housework and chores, their significant other's work-life balance, and communication. The one point that barely differs

by 1% are cohabiting partners and married couples' sex life satisfaction, which is an interesting observation.

2. Another insight the study provides is that there are key differences in why some couples choose to cohabit and why others choose to get married. One of them, as we discussed earlier, can be due to religious affiliations. The number one reason both married couples and cohabiting partners provide as their reason for choosing their method of the partnership are companionship and love. With married couples, the 'love' percentage is about 15% higher, while the companionship component between cohabitants and married couples is basically the same with a mere 5% difference. However, a more notable difference can be observed where four out of ten cohabiting partners add that cohabitation is easier on their pockets and it's a convenient arrangement—while 37%-38% of cohabiting partners cite this as a major contributing factor, only 10%-13% of married couples deem this to be a notable contributing factor. Cohabiting partners were the only individuals to identify testing their relationship as a reason to consider cohabiting, and about 23% thought that this is a good reason to see if things will work. On the contrary, roughly six out of ten married couples or 63% cited making a formal commitment as a major contributing factor in their decision to get hitched. A significant number of these couples who did not cohabit before getting married. A minimal number of couples decide to cohabit or get married because of a pregnancy, with both married and unmarried couples under 10%. However, the percentage of couples who married because they wanted to have children someday is significantly higher than those who decided on a cohabitation agreement; having children influenced about 31% of couples while cohabitation influenced 14% of couples.

3. Here is another interesting outcome to add to the mix: sixty-six percent of the married couples started their long-term relationship with cohabitation, as a first step towards marriage. These couples were also not engaged yet when they moved in together. A couple's level of education also appears to be a marker or an indicator towards whether cohabitation is going to lead to marriage or the intention of getting married. Cohabitors who are not engaged but have a college-level education at least, are more likely to see moving in together as a step towards getting married. If the partners both hold bachelor's degrees, there is a 50% chance of them having this intention. This probability slightly lessens with a college qualification to 43%, and if the couple holds a high school diploma or less, it drops to 28%. Even though these are the current statistics, that doesn't mean that these individuals don't have dreams of getting married. The statistics you just read may point to socio-economic and financial barriers that affect a couple's ability to have their dream life.

4. The fourth point links directly with the previous one, as many individuals, and two-thirds of cohabiters, say that one of the main reasons they can't get married, even though they want to, is because of either their own financial status or the financial status of their partner. Twenty-nine percent of cohabiters blame their own financial status and 27% of cohabiters blame their partner's financial status for not seeing marriage winking on their relationship horizon. For these individuals, making such a commitment that signifies the ultimate stability just doesn't feel right, and that may be an indication of how they view marriage itself and how highly they regard this commitment. About four out of ten individuals blame not being successful enough yet, or not reaching their job or financial goals that would make them feel prepared for marriage.

Opinions on Cohabitation, Partnerships, and Marriage: What Do Americans Say?

The younger generation of Americans are very optimistic about cohabitation as the majority of them regard this as a path that will eventually lead to marriage and a strong and steady relationship. To add to the numbers, 48% of American adults think that, if a couple lives together before getting married, their marriage will have a better success rate while only 13% think that living together before marriage will lead to a negative outcome. Then, you get the 38% who are completely indifferent, or so they say. A large part of adults that are optimistic about cohabitation before marriage is under the age of 30, while about a third of adults over the age of 30 think it doesn't make a difference.

The majority of Americans also think that cohabiting partners are just as able to raise healthy children as married couples. Just over 50% of cohabiting adults aged between 18 and 44 do have children or are busy raising children. Almost 60% of Americans think that whether a child is raised by cohabiting parents or by parents joined by marriage, this specific aspect will not affect the health of the child and that there are other, more important aspects to focus on than whether the parents' relationship is officiated or not. This then leaves the remaining 40% who say that it is better for a child to be raised by parents who are married. That leaves a teensy tiny, less than 1% who says they don't really care. Should we care? We should; however, we should also allow others to make their own decisions.

Americans show they care by expressing a majority view that cohabiting partners should have the same rights as married couples. These 'rights' refer to the legal preference married couples qualify for when getting health insurance when it comes to inheritance and other perks like tax benefits. Thirty-four percent of Americans think that these benefits should be exclusive to married couples as they went all the way and tied the knot, which can have some legal ramifications within itself, especially when things are not working out anymore. While a small percentage (approximately 16%-17% of American adults) think that marriage is essential for a successful relationship, a big chunk is more relaxed on the subject, as 54% say that marriage is definitely important, but it doesn't need to be essential. About the same percentage of Americans, 27%-28%, think that marriage is neither essential for a man or a woman to be able to live a fulfilling life; however, a much larger percentage believes that being in a romantic relationship is important for living life to the fullest.

*All statistics and studies have been sourced from the Pew Research Center (Menasce Horowitz et al., 2019).

Why Do Stats Matter?

Statistics are usually conducted on a control group, which needs to meet specific criteria. This is a requirement so that the research can provide balanced and accurate results because, you know, every single man, woman, and child on the planet cannot be interviewed and surveyed, and even if they could, it would be a laborious task to formulate those statistics because of every person's ability to be so unique. So, the information above is a good indication of what society's modern view about relationships and marriage is in general, but there can still be other views that did not surface in these statistics due to the fact that they are not completely mainstream in society. One of these would be the type of relationship Jean-Paul Sartre had with Simone de Beauvoir, because they weren't even cohabitants. However, these are the relationships individuals engage in: they move in together, they get married, but sometimes they just stay together without tying the knot. Along with this comes other details and preferences like whether they lived together before they were married and even contributing factors like finances. The important part or focal point is to keep each relationship, no matter where it is in its journey, healthy and productive and for both partners to feel fulfilled and wanted. These statistics gave us a glimpse not only of the general opinions of relationships and partnerships, but also the insecurities that may lie within an individual that they may or may not discuss with their partner, which may lead to communication issues and subsequent relationship obstacles. There are so many ways to approach and improve such a partnership, repair and maintain, and cherish and love. Before we start our discussion on how to heal, cherish, and maintain, let's see if there are any common issues that couples struggle with today and what they are.

The Biggest Long-Term Relationship Issues Today & 10 Reasons to Keep on Reading

There's a reason why people are looking for relationship advice. In many cases, couples are struggling with the same or similar issues, and if they are not the same, they may have the same roots. According to research, there are 11 obstacles that help long-term relationships like marriages stay afloat and stand the test of time. Some of them are external circumstances and some of them are related to one or both partners and their personal development. This section will not only point out the most common issues but may also help you identify some you can work on in your own relationship.

1. An issue that couples commonly experience when they've been together for a while or if they are in it for the long haul is that their goals tend to change, and this can change the alignment between their goals as a couple. When you started off, one of the reasons you felt that you were such a good match may have been because you shared many life goals. However, a lack of communication and life events can change this, and you may need some guidance to get back on track. Being a couple doesn't mean that you must have exactly the same goals, but it will make things easier if you are both moving in the same general direction.

2. Next is a dealbreaker for some but a situation that can be worked with for others: infidelity. Irrespective of how you feel about it personally, it is a major factor that affects long-term relationships and marriages. The infidelity itself is often just a symptom of a deeper issue that can be related to communication or expectations. Either way, there are ways to

work through infidelity and rebuild trust if both partners are willing to do so, and if the guilty party shows remorse.

3. There's a reason the mother-in-law stereotype exists, and this stereotype doesn't only represent the mother-in-law—it represents all family-related issues in this case. Believe it or not, unresolved family or in-law issues can cause serious problems in long-term relationships and marriages. Relationship issues are supposed to be between the two partners, so why would other family members wreak havoc in a long-standing relationship? There are several scenarios, of which the most popular would probably be the wife and mother-in-law not seeing eye-to-eye, both being too proud to back down, and the husband being stuck in the middle, too scared to tell whichever one who is overstepping the line to back off because he knows that, either way, there will be negative repercussions. However, family-related issues that cause relationship troubles come in all shapes and forms, and it can be from your twice-removed cousin's bedridden grandmother to your sister's new baby that are causing the issues. It all depends on the situation and the context.

4. Sex is always a hot topic when it comes to relationships. That's because it's a major component of any romantic partnership, and it links to various other constituents like trust, communication, and physical satisfaction. It is also a major reason why long-term relationships and marriages experience serious issues; however, most sexual issues can be worked through. Each case is of course individual, but sex with a long-term partner is not skin-deep, and it deserves to be looked at from a deeper perspective. Partners can often feel that they've become sexually incompatible. Sex-related issues can also be linked to a lack of intimacy between partners. These scenarios deserve a thorough analysis like any other relationship issue, I believe.

5. Very closely linked to sex-related issues are intimacy issues. Intimacy is not necessarily sexual, but it is one of the most essential components for a healthy romantic relationship. Thus, if the orchards of intimacy are barren and dry, the relationship is going to suffer significantly and bear little fruit. One often forgets that there is an emotional component to intimacy that partners tend to overlook, especially once the honeymoon phase is over and both partners become stuck in their daily grind. Moving too deep into your own life and too far away from the one you share with your partner is a common occurrence in today's life, and it has become one of the most common relationship problems.

6. The next one is one we've all experienced in relationships before, and that's arguing for the sake of arguing. Ineffective arguments that are not productive and not meant for the participants to reach a specific point of consensus can be hazardous for relationships, especially long-term relationships or marriages where couples have been going at each other for so long. You reach a point when arguing becomes a way to shut off your partner when you are faced with a difficult issue because you know that the method of argumentation is not productive or effective. Being on the defensive all the time is going to break down a relationship, and it seems like it has become a trend. You may not even have noticed that you're doing it until now, who knows?

7. If you've suddenly realized that you don't trust your partner with your life anymore, this can be the cause of serious relationship issues. When two people decide to get married or embark on a lifelong journey together, they usually have an agreement about trust and they share a deep connection based on mutual trust. When one or both partners start to experience a lack of trust after being together for a long time, it means that something must have happened along the way to damage this

trust relationship. One example is another point on this list, which is infidelity. However, there are many reasons why partners can start feeling betrayed; moreover, sometimes these feelings are suppressed, festering over time, and when the problem comes to light, the whole issue may be based on a misunderstanding or be blown completely out of proportion due to it not being addressed sooner. This is not always the case, though; sometimes partners betray each other where there will be a legitimate reason to feel distrustful. Whichever the case may be, trust issues are a major contributor to long-term relationship issues.

8. As you settle down with a partner and you start going through the motions, one of the phenomena that commonly start to manifest is a sometimes systematic and sometimes not-so-subtle tightening of boundaries from one partner or from both. Allowing your partner less freedom is going to incentivize them to either break the rules on purpose or do it behind your back. Why do boundaries suddenly start shifting to an unhealthy space for some couples when they've been together for a long time? This issue is a manifestation of a deeper problem that can be linked to trust, low self-esteem, or lingering issues from previous relationships that have not been dealt with sufficiently. For partners who value their freedom, these sudden restrictions can be a dealbreaker, and this is why unhealthy boundaries are such a common role-playing factor in relationship problems.

9. Is your relationship still fun? Do you still have fun, and do you still have the will to have fun with your partner? Many couples will answer a resounding 'no' to these questions. Losing the playful side of your bond is like losing a puzzle piece that completes the picture of ideal intimacy. It's hard to have fun when the stress keeps piling on, responsibilities loom over you like a never-ending pile of paperwork, and all you can remember from your day is waking up and going to bed. This is

one of the main issues in long-term relationships because this is how partners start drifting apart and start living separate lives under one roof. Is it fixable? You bet it is!

10. The final reason, which can tie into most of the previous common issues on the list, is when your partner-to-partner communication system is ineffective. Take for example a situation where partners ignore each other even though they know the other requires just a small sign of acknowledgment when they communicate. This is a subtle but clear sign of disrespect. Playing the ignoring-each-other game is almost like a type of power struggle between partners, very much like giving someone the silent treatment. One can imagine that this type of unwillingness to communicate clearly and effectively with one's partner can lead to serious relationship problems, as the partner receiving these messages of disrespect is most likely going to respond with retaliation, which will create a magnificent snowballing effect of hostility. Once the snowballing has reached a certain point, the 'un'-snowballing process can be difficult, depending on how much damage the relationship has suffered. However, if communication can cause relationship damage, then surely it should be able to offer a cure and emotional healing. It is the most versatile and effective relationship tool there is.

Do you see yourself and your relationship on this list? If so, how many times could you identify with it? Going through this identification process is important for effective problem-solving and learning techniques that can recreate the happiness and strong bond that may have been damaged through time, but even if you currently find nothing you can identify within this list, learning about a comprehensive approach towards relationship-building and healing is of immeasurable value and something you can always keep in your mind's back pocket.

Chapter 2:

Basic Communication

We're going to start with our journey by looking at one of the cornerstones of a successful relationship, which is communication. This concept is not only applicable to marriage but to every relationship you have and cherish in your life. Have you ever experienced a misunderstanding with someone that you love that affected your relationship negatively and maybe even permanently? Sometimes, we are so busy talking, gesturing, and demanding, that we don't realize how it comes across to the intended recipient. If the recipient of your information is the most important person in your life, revising your methods and approach can help you cultivate and prune a pretty, well-maintained love tree instead of one that looks like it has been through a hurricane. I may not even be referring to you; sometimes one partner works really hard on communicating effectively but the other just doesn't get it. You literally want to rip your hair out and say, "Listen, I am TRYING to open a channel of communication here that's non-judgmental and neutral. Can you just stop projecting?!" This has happened to me many times. Throughout our lives, we see people wanting to achieve things by means that ultimately cause conflict and resentment even if what they were trying to achieve wasn't so selfish in the first place. It's just a total disregard for effective communication. Once you know how much an open and productive communication process can help you in your relationship, you'll never want to turn back. However, it comes with a few T's and C's like accepting your partner for who they are. Now, that's a sign of true love.

The Art of Listening

Listening is one of the most important skills one needs to master for relationship maintenance and conflict resolution in a marriage. I think most of you will agree that a relationship always has a listener and a talker. What you need to do is tinker with this balance a bit. The listener can also spruce up their listening skills, but the talker, who usually doesn't know that they are a poor listener, needs to acknowledge that they need to develop their listening skills. The type of listening both parties need to aspire to is deep listening. Deep listening is an activity that requires the listener to do more than just absorb the information. It's a threefold process and consists of getting the information from your partner, making an effort to put yourself into the other person's shoes, and connect the information with an emotional experience. Being a proficient listener in a relationship is crucial because one thing we all have in common is that we want to be heard and understood, especially by the person who means the most to us

Another type of listening is active listening. If you want to apply active listening, you need to make that conscious decision that you are going to engage and absorb the information that is being presented to you. Active listeners perform this technique undistracted, which can provide your partner with a sense of assuredness that what they are telling you is important to you because your attention is undiverted. Be completely immersed in your partner's words and messages and indicate your interest by showing physical reassurance like nodding or maintaining eye contact. The two main types of listeners are characterized not only by their listening method but also by what their goal is and what they want to achieve by listening. First, you get individuals who listen to understand, and then you also get individuals who listen to respond. If a person is listening to respond, do you think that they are fully immersed in the listening process? Many of us are listeners that mostly focus on responding, but listeners who intend to understand are more likely to be satisfied in their relationship because they get more out of the communication process (Raab, 2017). What lays at the heart of these two types of listening? If you listen to understand, is it likely that you value your partner's feelings and contribution to the relationship and that you are more determined on fixing the issue? In contrast, if you listen to respond, are you possibly trying to avoid potential conflicting information from your partner and, while they are talking, you are using the time for retaliation or focusing on how to get your point across? If you've identified yourself as a "responder," this doesn't by any means indicate that you have bad intentions or that you are willfully trying to sabotage your relationship. This quality is deeply woven into how your listening skills developed; however, by identifying your listening type, you are that much closer to solving possible communication issues in your relationship.

Deep listening sits at the core of every healthy relationship because it encourages relationship growth and positive change. When you start to apply deep listening, you will get the most surprising response from your partner; they may have responded defensively in the past but are now more open and accepting because they can see that you are attentive and you care about their feelings. Who knows, they may even return the favor (Raab, 2017). Start with self-exploration. What goes through your mind when your partner is talking to you? Are you actively focusing on their words and placing yourself in their position, or are you formulating an award-winning response? Here's some great tips on how to improve your listening skills and ultimately your communication skills:

Dig into the words so you can listen for meaning, and try to place yourself in your partner's position to understand where they are coming from. Try not to judge and tend to the development of empathy in the listening process. You can learn a lot by observing your partner's body language and how it links to the verbal message you are getting. For example, are your partner's hands clasped together or balled into fists? This will indicate that they are frustrated or possibly angry, and you can work on understanding where this feeling comes from if you were not previously aware of it. The tone of voice and enunciation can help you understand which part of the message carries the most weight and which emotions you need to link with these words. If you want your partner's message to resonate to you personally, which is the most efficient way of understanding it, you can use empathetic reflection. This basically means that you need to take their words and repeat it to yourself in your own words, which will help you develop a common perspective. Finally, the best way you can let your partner know that you are processing their conversation is by regularly acknowledging using words like "yes" or "I understand" (you'll know what to say), and by summarizing parts of the conversation back to them that you can see are important and meaningful to them. Here, using empathetic reflection can be really useful (Raab, 2017).

Who's in Who's Shoes?

Ask yourself this important question: are you a "fixer?" Do you subconsciously want to fix your partner because you think that will fix the relationship? You see these fixers a lot: someone who married a smoker but now wants them to stop smoking. This tendency is actually related not to the faults you identify in your partner, but it is more likely a habit you developed because you have a need to influence and possibly control those around you. This is a great quality, especially in a career context, but in a relationship, this can cause miscommunication and emotional damage. Ask yourself if the problem you want to "fix" has always been a problem or if you developed the need for it to be a problem at a certain stage. Do your partner's jokes suddenly irritate you even though they've always been the same?

People's habits change over time, and sometimes partners become irritated with each other. You know, those classic "leaving the toilet seat up" or "not putting the cap on the toothpaste" kind of jokes you'd find in old movies. You see these tiny battles going on in relationships around you all the time, but sometimes you don't even notice that you're having the same battles in your own relationship. I've also witnessed some legitimate attempts at "fixing" happening in relationships, like when an ex-colleague of mine got pregnant but flatly refused to stop drinking and smoking and also made no attempt to seek help for possible addiction issues. This was really hard on her partner, and in this case, if you had to put yourself in her shoes, would you be able to identify a logical or productive reason for doing that? I mean, would you be able to empathize with her choices up to a point that would lead you to support them? Well, they eventually got divorced, the main reason unknown to me. However, I cannot help but think that her inability to put herself in her partner's shoes played a role in breaking their bond.

Let's also look at this from another perspective. If you were or are in a relationship with someone who has, for example, Bipolar Disorder, Unipolar Disorder, Schizoaffective Disorder, or any other related illness, how likely would you want to "fix" them? This is a completely different perspective because if you are in a relationship with someone who suffers from a mental illness, you witness their suffering. So, the reason you want to "fix" them is not only because it is incredibly hard for you to see someone you love so much struggle and experience that amount of pain, but you also want the best for them and you want them to lead a normal and happy life. Again, even in such a unique circumstance, "fixing" is not going to help your partner. In this case, it is extremely difficult—I would say impossible—to put yourself in their shoes, and deep listening, open communication, and unconditional support is what will get your partner through the deepest of waters. This does not mean that if your partner suffers from any other type of illness that it will be easier. You also cannot put yourself in someone's shoes who has been diagnosed with cancer. Trying to put yourself in your partner's position instead of trying to "fix" them from your own perspective is an act of true love and selflessness. This act will awaken healthy communication and understanding between partners, which is the basis of a prosperous and long-lasting relationship.

The Impact of Your Voice

Intonation is something we don't really notice or focus on when communicating, except when we're literally shouting or whispering. While you are happily chatting away, your intonation paints a clear picture of the intentions and emotions behind your words to those who listen closely. When used intentionally, it can also inspire the wanted response from the individual you are communicating with, like when you are talking to your partner. For example, you can say a simple phrase like "The sun is shining" in so many different ways. This means that your tone or intonation can indicate to the listener whether you are happy about the sun shining or whether you are holding the sun in contempt because you forgot your sunblock. You can even use a gossipy tone. Just make sure the sun doesn't hear you.

From this perspective, you can probably just imagine how many hidden messages there can be identified in a passionate argument between two lovers. Do they pick them up? Some you do, some you don't. But, never underestimate their ears and the subconscious messages they send to your brain. Just saying.

According to a study conducted by the University of California, where researchers observed the tone of the voices of couples in therapy sessions, they came to the shocking conclusion that the therapists' opinions and predictions about whether the marriage will last were a less successful predictor than when the couples' tone of voice was used. The study was conducted over a period of two years and a computer algorithm was used to analyze the tonality in the voices. I wonder if this same algorithm could tell if the therapist was any good. Even more mind-blowing evidence from this study is that it included a follow-up after five years where the algorithm was involved in predicting the relationship status of these couples; did the relationships that were still intact improve or deteriorate? Based on the analysis of voice tonality, the algorithm was able to make a 74% accurate prediction (Gersho, n.d.).

When communicating in general, you must consider your tone of voice to be one of the most influential aspects of how you present your message. So, just imagine how important tone of voice is when you are having a serious discussion with your partner. Your tone of voice can give both conscious and subconscious messages to the listener, and factors that influence your tone of voice are timbre, speed, volume, projection, and clarity. Your tone of voice is regarded as part of the nonverbal factors of communication, and it is also seen as important because your genuine feelings or intentions can easily shine through your tone, regardless of your words. Have you ever seen a movie that's in a foreign language where you couldn't understand the words *per se*, but you could understand the tone and nature of a relationship between characters just by how they talk to each other? This is a great example of how tone is a dead giveaway of a speaker's true intentions. Moreover, focusing on your tone, conscious, and subconscious when you are having a serious discussion with your partner can help to navigate clear communication channels.

How can you improve your relationship and communication with your partner just by rethinking your tone of voice? Do you think that taking a quick pause before responding in a sarcastic tone and swapping it for a gentler and patient one can make a difference in your relationship? Don't make that a gentle and overly patient tone that translates back to sarcasm, though; then you'll be back where you started. That one moment of frustration you experience with your partner is not going to last, but by expressing it whilst communicating may have a lasting effect on your partner. If you recognize that you or your partner have a knack for not focusing on your voice tones and this tends to heat up a conversation into a full-blown argument, you can focus on doing the following:

Pay close attention to how your tone of voice changes when it is linked to specific behaviors or comments made by your partner. Stay observant of your tone of voice, even if you are speaking to others. This will cultivate a heightened awareness that you can use to improve communication with others as well as with your partner. You can also try and analyze something that you said. What was the dominant tone that you think the listener would pick up and interpret? Also, what do you think were the more subtle tones they may have picked up subconsciously? You can follow these observations by asking yourself how you could have improved the message by possibly changing your tone. What you say forms the basis of your message, but how you say it is going to determine the effect it has on your listener (Gersho, n.d.).

Body Language

Body language is also a form of non-verbal communication that plays an almost more pivotal role in communication. There are specific types of body language that have been identified to play an important role in healthy relationships and also other types that can cause the deterioration of a relationship. Let's first look at the role body language plays in communication, especially in more intimate relationships, and then move forward to focus on types of constructive and destructive body language.

Body language is the physical behavior and mannerisms you emanate while using other forms of communication like speech, which can reveal more details about your message nonverbally. Body language can be either intentional or unintentional (Segal et al., 2019). The thing that makes body language so interesting is that a person's body language can refute or contradict the content of their verbal communication and show their true intentions. Nonverbal communication happens continuously while we communicate with others, whether we are aware of it or not. It's surprising how many aspects of your body can send nonverbal messages to others: these include your hand gestures, your posture, how you position your legs and arms when you sit or stand, and eye contact. As we mentioned earlier, your tone of voice also forms part of nonverbal communication but not necessarily body language. Let's look at a general example. Your body language, whether intentional or unintentional, can be used to build relationships and trust and to connect with others. However, it can also offend and alienate others or be just plain confusing. You should also keep in mind that body language is not only active or effective when you are talking; it is still active even when you are silent and you don't intend to communicate directly with anyone. Think of it as a broadcaster of your true intentions and feelings (Segal et al., 2019).

Nonverbal communication like body language is crucial, especially in relationships, because they can tell your partner how much you're invested in the relationship without you even saying a word. If your body language is not in line with what you are verbally communicating, this can arouse suspicion and trust issues with your partner. If this does happen, you may also need to ask yourself why these contradicting messages happen. Here are some common body language cues that indicate disinterest or a wedge that may be growing between you and your partner.

When you speak to your partner, do they stand or sit with their feet pointing towards you or away from you? Even their upper body can be turned away as if they want to deflect your attempt to communicate. A partner that is interested in your feelings and that wants to commit to the relationship will most likely show this by sitting attentively with their body pointing straight at yours. If your partner tends to bite their lip when you're having a serious discussion, there may be reason to believe that they are holding back information, feelings, or cropped-up emotions that they don't want to reveal to you. Another behavioral trait that links with feet and an upper body that are turned away is when your partner crosses their legs. This may be a habit of theirs, but take note if they do this while you are having a serious conversation. This nonverbal cue is almost like a defensive message that says, "I am unavailable and don't want to open up for a constructive conversation." This gesture is completely subconscious, which according to psychologists, makes it so telling. The crossing of arms is very similar to the exposure of the stomach to another individual and is a psychological indication of developing trust. If your partner crosses their arms, especially if you are having a serious or deep conversation, it is a definite indication of a "no entry" sign. It is, just like the crossing of the legs, associated with a defensive stance as the individual does not want to expose themselves to the other party. Have you noticed how people tend to cross their arms when they are angry or when they are being confronted? You can calm down your partner by using a gentle approach if you are instigating the discussion to see if that works (Greenwald, 2019).

Observe your partner's smile closely. Can you detect genuine enthusiasm, and is it alive with positive emotion? Alternatively, is your partner's smile a bit on the uncomfortable side, and does it make you feel unsettled? Although these are general themes one should look out for, I feel that I should also add that there may be exceptions to the rule. For example, if your partner is suffering from debilitating depression, it may be hard for them to smile. However, you may find the genuineness you are seeking in their eyes. So, when you use these researched tips as a guideline for constructive communication, ensure that you apply it within the context of your relationship to make it functional.

Next, there's the eye contact enigma. Is your partner mostly avoiding eye contact or are they making eye contact all the time, to the point that you may feel something weird is going on? Both can be warning signs. If your partner avoids eye contact, it can indicate that they are emotionally disconnected and disinterested. It may even suggest dishonesty as they don't want you to detect this in their eyes. Conversely, your partner may be overly conscious of the fact that they are likely avoiding making eye contact and they might try to overcompensate (Greenwald, 2019). If your partner tends to do this, you can use the opportunity to look into their eyes for possible clues and indications of how they are feeling. Are they trying too hard? Additionally, does it look like they are trying to hide something? If they do choose to make eye contact but it doesn't feel completely right, take the opportunity to see if there are any warning signs.

How does your partner's choice of proximity make you feel? For example, do they prefer to sit close to you on your three seater, or do they sit on the other end or even on the chair next to the sofa? You don't have to cuddle each other every single minute of the day, but if there is a complete absence of this need to be close, it may indicate that you don't feel the same about things. This is a really difficult situation because, if your partner starts to show this behavior, trying harder to maintain that closeness is going to be perceived as clinginess and excessive neediness. The best way to approach this if you pick up this behavior is to have an honest conversation. In contrast, if your partner does make physical contact with you but it is restricted to just patting you on the back, this is a giveaway that the romantic component in your relationship is undergoing strain. There's nothing wrong with a teasing pat on the back or even a genuine one, but your closeness shouldn't end there. It is a way of showing that your partner is moving towards deromanticizing and desexualizing your relationship.

Is your partner giving you an enveloping hug or are they keeping their elbows locked and drawn back? We all want to be in a tight and loving embrace with our partner, especially if we need emotional support. However, if your partner hugs you but still tries to keep their distance, you need to ask yourself why they act so reserved. Does your partner appear to want to limit physical contact with you even though it is obvious that you need it? Except if they are also experiencing a really bad time or there may be some other reason why they feel detached, you can keep this form of nonverbal communication in the back of your mind for further observation (Greenwald, 2019).

Now that we've looked at nonverbal communication, specifically body language, and we've focused on warning signs through negative body language, what are the positive counterparts? The following examples are ones you can implement in constructive conversations with your partner to improve overall communication and relationship building.

Let's start with maintaining meaningful eye contact that shows your interest in what your partner is saying. In other words, the opposite of avoiding or forcing eye contact. I don't know if you agree with me, but the eyes are truly windows to the soul, and if you know your partner well and they know you well, they will pick up how much their feelings mean to you. This, in turn, will give them the confidence to be honest, which will make relationship building and solving problems so much easier. It is such a simple gesture. Combine meaningful eye contact with deep listening and apply what you see in your partner's eyes to their words and tone of voice.

Next, open up your body and show your partner that you trust them enough to be vulnerable in their presence. Doing the opposite like crossing your arms and legs and turning away your body from your partner most likely happens without you noticing, but you can make a conscious effort to change that. Make sure that your feet both point directly to your partner, which will bring your whole body to face in that direction. Place your hands on your lap or on arm rests if they are available and avoid clenching your fists. Uncross your legs if you've already crossed them out of habit. Expose yourself. You may just encourage your partner to do the same by making them feel more at ease and willing to open up. If you've noticed that your partner has been having issues with proximity, don't sit on their lap, but don't sit too far away. Show them that you want to be close, but you are also giving them space. Evaluate your partner's body language carefully. Do they need a hug? Do they need you to hold their hand? Alternatively, do they need you to just listen and provide support from a distance? If you identify any body language from your partner that we mentioned and discussed above, your best first move is to counter it gently with positive body language. Confronting them aggressively will cause conflict as they may not even be aware of the fact that they are exhibiting these telling signs.

If you experience negative body language from your partner while you are communicating, you can start by seeking clarity or looking for the reason why they may be acting this way. If you cannot find the answers you are looking for yourself, try giving your partner a gentle nudge by saying something like, "I got the feeling that you were not completely comfortable with the words I used when I explained how I felt yesterday." Follow up your prompt with a question that allows them to express themselves. Use a simple cue like, "How did it make you feel?" Or, if you want to be a bit more specific, try, "Did the way I said X and Y sound too harsh?" By being neutral and non-judgmental, you can help your partner open up to discover the feelings they were showing through their body language. It is crucial to remember here that, if you want to communicate clearly from your side, you need to be focused on your own body language and try to emanate positive and appropriate body language faultlessly. Nobody's perfect, but if your body language mirrors your partner's, you are not likely to get the answers you want or contribute positively to relationship-building (Beohm, 2018).

A crucial detail to place at the back of your mind and always remind yourself about is that even though you may be witnessing what appears to be negative body language, you are not a mind reader and you shouldn't come to conclusions on your own. It is important to know what contributed to your partner's behavior and if it also includes factors that are not you. This also ties into an important approach you should avoid when dealing with negative body language: don't communicate your concerns in a way that makes it look like it's all about you (Beohm, 2018).

Finally, the more aware you are of your own body language and aim to keep it clear and consistent with other methods of communication, the less negative energy you are likely to attract from others. Let's call it reactive energy and body language. As the final part of this chapter, we're going to look at the difference between proactive and reactive behavior and the extensively adverse effects these behaviors can have on a relationship.

Proactivity Versus Reactivity

Proactivity and Reactivity describe the way individuals perceive, react, and base their feelings on things. For example, a proactive individual has the ability to make constructive decisions even in dire circumstances and are known to act as opposed to waiting for someone else to act first. A reactive individual is more dependent on and influenced by their circumstances, and they are not known for taking initiative or the first step. As you can imagine, having two reactive types in a relationship can come down to a lot of conflict and misunderstanding because both parties are influenced by their environment and are more likely to react emotionally to external stress without feeling the need to fix it. Reactive behavior can be toxic in a relationship, and it can manifest in verbal and non-verbal communication as well as decision-making.

A reactive individual can be bothered and influenced by external factors like what others say about them, the mood the people around them are in, if their children are being disobedient, if their partner is in a bad mood, and even a misinterpreted comment that they perceived to be an insult. This happens because reactivity causes the body to flood with the stress hormone cortisol, which activates the "fight or flight" action. Therefore, your reactions are not based on rationalizations created in your brain anymore but become an immediate defensive and often aggressive reaction due to your body's defense mechanisms. As you read this, you've probably realized that we all have some level of reactivity in us because life is so stressful. However, one needs to come to a point of asking, "Is it constructive and is it healthy?" Proactive behavior doesn't come as naturally, but it can be developed and will do wonders for communication in your relationship.

Proactive thinking and behavior are based on staying emotionally unaffected by what's happening around you. Proactivity is practiced by blocking out external factors and choosing how you want to think or act regardless with the aim to obtain the best results. So, proactive behavior is not about changing those around you but changing how external stimuli affect you when you decide to react or behave in a certain way. Create breathing space between your inner self and your external environment. This can help you to choose what you need to focus on, what your priorities are, and how your actions can be most beneficial during communication with your partner (Brandt, 2018).

Developing a proactive mindset will also make you a happier person because you are not so dependent on your environment to dictate how you should feel. This mindset is linked to an internal "locus of control," which means that you as an individual hold yourself responsible for your actions and you don't tend to blame others for your failures. You also feel responsible for your successes because, as a proactive individual, you most likely have a majority share in them. However, if your locus of control is external and not internal, you will gravitate towards reactive behavior, which includes blaming others and not being willing to take responsibility for situations you are in. This goes back to being ruled by your environment instead of depending on your own abilities (Brandt, 2018). Relationships are about give and take; however, one can't always be the giver and the other be the taker. A proactive mindset is a giving mindset, and a reactive mindset is a taking mindset. Are you a giver or a taker? And more importantly, do you want to be a giver or a taker? Because we are naturally inclined to take, focus on giving. For example, when your partner comes home after work looking angry and upset, be proactive by making them a cup of coffee or pouring them a glass of wine instead of being instantly irritated with their mood. After a glass or two, you'll definitely know why they came in looking like that.

Chapter 3:

The 5 Love Languages

Have you ever dated someone and felt that you understood their wants and needs very well and then dated someone else and later realized that this person may be from another planet? This phenomenon can be attributed to the different ways individuals experience affection and love, which has been coined the *Love Languages* by Dr. Gary Chapman, who started his early career as a marriage counselor. Chapman was good at his job as he was very observant, and after numerous sessions with couples who were experiencing conflict in their relationships, he noticed that there is a golden string that ran through all of these couples' situations, even though they were all unique. The issue would come down to one partner not feeling loved by the other, and the other being so frustrated because they don't know how to show their love "correctly," while this love is there and while it is abundant and sincere. What a terrible misunderstanding, and what an absolute tragedy if a relationship would end up on the rocks because of this. Even more interesting, Chapman found that, if a spouse feels that their partner doesn't love them, the specific needs they have to feel loved always seem to fall into one of five categories. These became the 5 love languages and identifying your own love language and that of your partner can significantly improve the way both of you feel in your relationship when it comes to security, trust, understanding, and open communication (Moody, LaCroix Design Co, 2019).

Who is Dr. Gary Chapman?

Chapman, as we just established, is the attentive marriage counselor who noticed the similarities between the couples' marital issues who came to see him since his early career days. His early career days are more than a quarter of a century ago, and since then, the concept of the 5 love languages has become famous and helped scores of couples understand the way they show and receive love in their relationships. Chapman's theory has a simple premise that can be applied to the most diverse types of relationships and personality types. The premise is that we are all different, and we have different personalities. Therefore, we are bound to express love in different ways and experience it in different ways.

Dr. Gary Chapman, Ph.D., is now an established and famous author, speaker, and still a sought-after counselor. He directs marriage seminars, and his book, *The 5 Love Languages,* has sold over 12 million copies, stayed at the top of numerous reputable literary charts for subsequent years, and he also has a national radio program that airs on over 400 stations. If you don't know anything about the 5 love languages, you must be itching by now to know what they are, never mind which one you are. I wonder if you'll be able to make an accurate guess by just looking at them. Here they are: the 5 lifesaving love languages that help save and are still helping to save so many relationships are *Words of Affirmation, Acts of Service, Receiving Gifts, Quality Time,* and—you can't leave this one out—*Physical Touch.* When you look at these five languages, which have been so aptly categorized according to human nature and relationships, it is possible that you may have an epiphany right away by realizing what's missing in your relationship. However, it's not always that simple, and for those cases, there's a quiz you can take that will help you to find your dominant love language. Even if you do have an inkling, taking the quiz may be the best way to make sure, because you may end up having more than one prominent love language, and who knows, you may even have one that you haven't really been aware of all of this time (Moody, LaCroix Design Co, 2019).

The Quiz You Need to Take

You can gain easy access to the quiz by just looking for it on your search engine. You'll notice that there are different love language quizzes as the theory has progressed; there is now a quiz for children, teenagers, and this theory can even be used in the workplace to improve employee relations. However, we are looking at the relationship quiz. The quiz will ask you a few preliminary questions like your gender and age, and then you will officially start by having two choices that contain scenarios between you and your partner, and you need to choose the one you prefer. For example, you may have to choose between your partner bringing you a small gift when they get home from work every day and your partner verbally complimenting you. This, of course, is just an example and is not necessarily a choice you'll have to make when taking the quiz. In some cases, you may get options where it's really difficult to choose, and in these cases, it's best to go with your gut. Which one felt right first, and which one felt right after you thought about it a little more? The one that felt right first is probably the one that reflects your true relationship needs the best. In the end, you will most likely have all of these languages jumbled together in your assembled love language, but there will be certain languages that will stand out above the rest. These are the ones that are most important to you.

The First Love Language: Words of Affirmation

The first clue one can usually get, but not necessarily the most important or only indicator that you or your partner's love language is words of affirmation is that you are careful and good with words, written and spoken. This indicates a primary love for language, which is often linked to this love language.

The best way to describe words of affirmation is as an act to uplift, confirm, support, or to genuinely empathize with your significant other from an angle of positivity. This is a way of showing love, and it is some individual's most rewarding way of receiving love from their partner. If you have a partner who has words of affirmation as a high-ranking love language, you can understand their need by thinking of it this way: in general, words are important to them and really impact them emotionally, as it speaks to the emotional voice they use inside to express themselves and to experience emotions. Imagine now that one partner has this need and the other has no idea. One can just sense the feeling of emptiness that can start developing if your partner doesn't use words to express their love for you, not even in the simplest expression. Examples of words of affirmation that can change your partner's world are *you inspire me, I am grateful for you, I'm proud of you, I love you, you are special to me,* and *I appreciate it when you...*

People who prioritize words of affirmation as their love language often have a deeper need for verbal affirmation, positive reinforcement, and they may need acknowledgment in the form of compliments and praise to feel worthy, not necessarily only as a person, but as your partner. This may be hard to understand for partners who have words of affirmation at the bottom of their love language list, so here's where it becomes important to conscientiously put yourself in your partner's shoes, and vice versa. These words can have an indescribable effect of fulfillment and gratification on your partner, and they will return the favor in the best way they can. Appreciation is at the heart of this love language, but the method of communication is also significant.

Take note that if you've just realized that your partner's love language is indeed words of affirmation and you want to start vocalizing your feelings more, if you're going to sound rehearsed, then it will have the opposite effect. An integral part of these expressions is their sincerity and spontaneity, almost as if your partner has been on your mind all day and you couldn't wait to tell them how you feel. Or it's like you're experiencing a passionate or emotional moment and you felt the need to let them know in a language they appreciate. Develop a habit of expressing yourself verbally whenever you have a positive feeling about your partner. Make sure that there's no duality or a dichotomy lurking in what you're saying. For example, *you look so beautiful today, I think you should throw away the dress you wore yesterday.* This is an awful example, but you get the idea, right? It kind of sounds like something a husband would say to his wife on a '90s sitcom. So, there you have it. Avoid the '90s sitcom approach and focus on being sincere and being honest when you express yourself verbally. Here are your best tips if your partner gushes about words of affirmation.

1. Don't do it once a month. Also, don't do it every half hour. But do it often. The best way to approach this love language is to say the positive things that pop up in your mind. If there are none, you definitely have to read the rest of the book, but don't worry, you'll get to that point. Think about your partner having a love tank, and every time you speak their love language, you are putting fuel into their tank that keeps them going and making your relationship stronger. The more you focus on keeping them fueled with their love language, the more receptive and open they will be in your relationship.

2. It's important to keep in mind that, just like you can have a slip-up and say something ambiguous instead of saying something positive like we mentioned earlier, positive language and affirmations will not have the desired effect if they are alternated with tactless critique, ridicule, or any other insensitive remarks. This doesn't mean that you can now never give your opinion on anything your partner does ever again, but if words are important to them, then all words are important. However, because you are in an intimate relationship with this person who appreciates words of affirmation, special messages, compliments, reassurance, and empathy that you express verbally, these will form part of the glue that keeps you together. What I'm ultimately saying is that words of affirmation is a big-picture approach. It goes specific, and it goes broad-spectrum.

3. Some of us are not, well, well-versed. You know, verbally talented. So, even though your partner may have words of affirmation as their dominant love language, you may not be a wordsmith or even just somebody who normally uses words as

a form of expressing yourself. If this is the case, your partner is surely aware of it, and you can use writing as a form of communication. Sometimes, compromises need to be made, and if your partner understands, they will appreciate a love note hidden between the last pages they read in their current bedside page-turner just as much as a sincere "I love you" or "I missed you today." If alterations need to be made so the need can be fulfilled, then come to a compromise that you both feel comfortable with (Nguyen & Jacobs Hendel, 2020).

The Second Love Language: Acts of Service

Acts of Service is the second of the 5 love languages, and it differs greatly from the first (words of affirmation). The most notable way in which it differs from the first one is that there is no verbality required. A person whose main love language is acts of service is someone who finds deep appreciation in the expression of a thoughtful gesture from their partner. It essentially means that you will go out of your way to do something for your partner or to show support, even when you're busy with something else. An act of service can make its receiver feel safe, cared for, appreciated, and loved, which is what we all want out of an intimate relationship in the end.

You can look at acts of service as an "actions speak louder than words" kind of love language. So, if this is your partner's love language and you're not really a talker, it's your lucky day. The physical act is where the value lies, and the effort put into it to help your partner or lessen their burden is of priceless value to them.

Yes, acts of service can be doing the laundry when your partner is too busy or picking up the kids from school, or even cooking a surprise dinner. There's also a tricky part to this love language to master if your partner speaks "acts of service." In essence, your approach and your acts should show that you understand the innermost wants and needs of your partner on an emotional level as well as helping them out with the more general tasks in life. You can even go as far as to say that an act of service that would have a lasting effect on your partner is one that shows accommodation to your partner's innermost desires. Here are a few examples of acts of service that would satisfy needs that are on different levels:

- Choose to do their favorite date activity, even if you don't necessarily like it.
- Prepare clean sheets and bedding after your partner's had a long day at work.
- Pay special attention to them and look after them when they are sick.
- Bring them coffee in bed.
- Get them that item they've been eyeing for a while but still couldn't get themselves to buy.
- When tidying up their personal space, place all their things in the exact place they prefer them to be.
- Show genuine interest in an activity or hobby they're involved in by attending an event or a class with them or initiating a thought-provoking discussion that shows you're interested in their interests.
- Play their favorite music without them asking you to put it on.

These are just general examples, and some of them may not apply to your relationship. An effective way to find out how you can make the most of your partner's love language is to observe them, observe their routines, and to listen to what they say, as their hidden desires are often written between these words. To make this easier for you too, let these acts of service sync with your own schedule by thinking of your partner as you go through your day. There will always be some ways you can show them how much you love them in a practical, non-verbal gesture they'll find most meaningful. If you are getting started on trying out this method with your partner, consider these basic guidelines that will lead you to make good decisions that will lead to successful acts of service.

1. Anticipate their wants and especially their needs by following a creative approach. For example, you don't necessarily have to only look out for current needs. You can also be creative by looking at future needs. What does my partner always forget when they get in the car on their way to work? Instead of them getting out again and messing up the kitchen looking for their entrance card, place it on their car seat beforehand. By applying yourself and focusing on this aspect conscientiously in the beginning, you'll develop a natural tendency to identify deeper needs versus more day-to-day needs and which ones your partner will appreciate most at what time.

2. Listening skills always come in handy. You can identify what your partner wants you to do for them by simply listening. They're not going to ask for it directly, but you'll find your answers when they express themselves openly in normal conversations you have as a couple. For example, do they complain a lot about something? Do they frequently talk about something specific? These things occur subconsciously, but it can reveal a lot about what they need for fulfillment, and lucky you, all you have to do is let the information enter your ears and allow your mind to process it.

3. If you are the lucky one who is on the receiving end, it is crucial that you show your partner the necessary appreciation and gratitude when they render these acts of service. I imagine that this won't be hard if your primary love language is acts of service because their efforts will make you genuinely happy and will be meaningful. So, remember to show it so you don't discourage your partner's efforts. Even better, if you can incorporate your partner's love language in these expressions of gratitude, there will be little hearts floating around all day.

4. Don't make this hard on yourself. When deciding how you want to approach these acts of service, they don't need to fall outside your budget, skill set, vocal range, or anything else you

plan to use in the process. This is something your partner also needs to understand. If they expect something from you that you can't give them because you are not superman, then you need to have a heart-to-heart. This being said, don't consider yourself and your skills limited or your abilities undevelopable. The sky's the limit. Find your balance.

5. Because your partner is specifically focused on acts of service, not following through on a commitment or promise is a massive no-no. This can not only damage the relationship, but it can break the trust between you completely, depending on what the commitment was. Even if it was a small commitment that you, personally, see as insignificant, like going out to dinner on Thursday, your partner is going to remember if you don't follow through. If they start to identify a pattern, this can cause serious trust issues even if you carry out other acts of service. This is your heads up. Keep commitments with your partner a priority, no matter how small, because you never know—they are likely keeping tabs.

If you are not sure what kind of acts of service will make your partner happy and you can't find those answers in their verbal or non-verbal communication, it's always a good idea to have a straightforward conversation. Tell your partner that you want to make them happy and this is a priority for you, so you want to do it right. If you need to talk about this, also keep in mind that talking about it once may not be enough because you and your partner's wants and needs evolve as time goes on. So, maintain and nurture the conversation and make it part of your acts of service ritual. As soon as you know what they need, you can give this to them in a genuine way, instead of guessing and not adding that essential, heartfelt element (Nguyen, 2020).

The Third Love Language: Receiving Gifts

Most people would interpret this love language as a materialistic need for diamond rings, expensive attire, and other costly items. This is one of the reasons why the love language "receiving gifts" is the most misunderstood love language, and if this is your partner's dominant love language, it's worth reading this section. Many partners read "receiving gifts" only and immediately the words 'materialistic' or 'greedy' pops into your head without warning. That's why it's important—if this is your initial reaction—to make a conscious mind shift. The type of person whose primary love language is giving gifts is not interested in extravagance or expensive gifts; they are the sentimental kind. Of course, for someone to be sentimental about something and keep it as a souvenir, it usually needs to be a tangible item, but it needn't be expensive, and that's where the misconception lies. The gift should be more about meaning, a token of love, or a small souvenir or reminder of a special time you spent together. What this essentially means is that an individual with this primary love language is not as shallow as you may have thought, and if you are used to the extravagant approach, doing this the right way may be harder than you think. Luckily, there's always that thing called learning! Let's begin with the basics of pleasing your not-so-shallow-after-all, gift-loving gem of a partner.

Knowing your partner and the way they view life is crucial to your gift-giving approach. One of the key components of relationships that will always remain unchanged (and its significance is illustrated through its reiteration) is that we, as humans, have similarities, but we remain individuals. We view life through our individualized lenses, and by knowing and understanding the color of your partner's lens, you can add meaning and value to your approach to their love language.

You can focus on giving large gifts every now and again if you want, but you'll be surprised to see that it's those small, thoughtful gifts that really light up your partner's eyes. In a way, it's the same as an act of service, except, you provide a token of your love and devotion that your partner can physically touch, even if they're going to eat it (food can also be a gift). If you are not sure if your partner's primary love language is receiving gifts and you want to look for signs without them taking the official quiz, you can study their reaction when presenting them with a gift. The act of gift-giving can either unlock an embarrassed-like reaction if your partner feels slightly uncomfortable with the material aspect of receiving a gift, but if your partner gushes about it, immediately wears it, puts it on display, immediately eats it or saves it for a special occasion but still tells all their friends about it, then you know you've hit the spot. If this tactic doesn't work or if you don't get a clear reaction, which can also happen, you can always just ask (Gould & Blackburn, 2020).

The Fourth Love Language: Quality Time

So, how would you know your partner has a quality time soul? Everyone needs some quality time and everyone needs some time apart. However, if your partner's primary love language is quality time, they likely see time as something extremely valuable, irreplaceable, and, from a relationship perspective, something that must be cherished. They may be the one who always wants to take a picture to remember a special moment, and while they appreciate other manifestations of love and affection, none come close to spending time with the one they love most.

But what is quality time, and how does your partner define this concept that means so much to them? This is one of the most important aspects of getting quality time with your partner right and making them feel cherished and loved the way you want to. The first, most important thing to understand about quality time as a love language is that being in the same place at the same time does not necessarily equate to quality time; in fact, it rarely makes the cut. It's a great start, though, if you are not in a situation where you cannot be together at that specific time. So, let's start there. We've established that location does not automatically equal the quality in quality time. The quality aspect in this love language is closely related to attentiveness and focusing on your partner alone instead of sitting next to your partner but dividing your attention between other individuals who are also present or texting someone. Here are a few indicators that your partner's primary love language may be quality time based on their own habits and behavior:

- Your partner is naturally attentive and a good listener. When they are with you, they give you their undivided attention and focus on what's going on between the two of you.
- Your partner finds it easy to focus and can block out distractions without any trouble.
- They value experiences over gifts or favors.
- If your partner enjoys spending time with people instead of being alone and are more extroverted than introverted, they are more likely to value quality time. However, this does not mean that individuals whose primary love language is quality time are always extroverts.
- It's a giveaway if your partner not only makes time for others in their life but enjoys doing it—even if their friends and family are not physically with them.

As we've established several times, other ways to find out is by either taking the quiz (recommended) or asking. Now, after you've secured this information, you need to find ways to show your partner that you love them using quality time in a way they would most appreciate. What does your partner like to do? For example, you can start by looking at activities, as quality time translates most successfully into spending time in close proximity while doing something enjoyable. This may be your most practical option. It's when you and your partner are spending time away from each other when you may have to be more creative. A great thing about quality time is that it doesn't need to be anything extravagant like you jumping out of a giant cake and then preparing a special lunch. In fact, that's exactly not the point. Consider ideas like taking a walk with your partner around the block or in the neighborhood where you live and give them your undivided attention. Focus on the moment, your time together, and what your partner is saying to you. If your partner enjoys social events, you can go out to a concert or have dinner somewhere and enjoy the movement around you while staying in your quality time bubble. When you're at home, get out your partner's favorite board game and have some fun. Even if it's Scrabble and you can't cheat because you're not playing on an app linked with a special compatible cheat app you pre-installed.

Quality time is a lot like couples' self-care, which you'll read about more in Chapter 7. This is because not only is spending quality time with your partner such a productive and healthy thing to do, but you can also choose to do it in a healthy and productive way, like going for a run together or preparing a healthy and delicious meal together. You can approach quality time plans from a long-term and short-term outlook by taking a walk (short-term) or by planning and taking on a new project together that will take some time to finish, like training for an annual marathon (long-term). If you do both short and long-term quality time together, not only will the partner whose primary love language is quality time benefit—a combination of these types of activities will create a rock-solid foundation for your relationship and bring both of you so much closer together. Everyone can learn something from this love language; although quality time has an extra special place in some people's hearts, the mindful practice thereof is extra important for all relationships and also for individuals who are native speakers of one of the other four love languages (Benninger, 2019).

The Fifth Love Language: Physical Touch

Physical touch is another love language with a little bit of a stigma around it. Like the receiving gifts misconception, people who are not familiar with the 5 love languages tend to think that physical touch is purely sexual and about desire and lust. This is, in fact, not the case. In many cases, sexual arousal is the last thing on someone's mind whose physical touch calls are not being answered by their partner. It may even lead to repulsion. Let me explain.

The language of physical touch is based on a deeper yearning for feeling safe and being acknowledged or being seen. These 'touches' are not overtly sexual in nature but more affectionate and protective, and they can even be territorial, like when a woman places her hand on her partner's chest. Examples of physical touch are when couples hold hands, when an individual puts their arm around their partner's shoulder, the touch of a shoulder or arm when interacting, the squeeze of a hand, and a kiss on the forehead. There are many more, but these should be an adequate illustration, I think.

If you know that your partner's primary love language is physical touch, there is one very important thing you need to know, and this is that they still need you to respect their personal space. In other words, they will show you when they are open to affection, and when you should leave them alone. This is not to make things harder for you but should rather just be seen as a normal form of self-preservation. Your partner's primary love language is most likely physical touch if the following characteristics or behaviors remind you of them:

- Your partner is either comfortable with or also enjoys public displays of affection (PDA's), whether it be among people you know or larger groups.
- They have expressed to you in the past or you get the feeling that they feel alone and isolated if they don't get regular affection from you.
- Massages, foot rubs, and neck rubs are better than expensive wine and chocolate.
- They always sit close to you, and they give the best, warmest, and most affectionate hugs.
- They often touch others subtly when they talk to them on the arm, shoulder, or even the face if they know them well.

The love language of physical touch is easy to understand, so it is also easy to learn, especially if you know your partner well. You'll be able to see when your partner is open to affection in their facial expression and sometimes also in the way their hands are placed on or against their body. For example, if your partner's hands are on their hips, they are most likely upset and need their space. However, you will also be able to pick this up by looking at their face. Consider these easy ways to show physical affection in ways that your partner is guaranteed to appreciate:

1. Holding your partner's hand means something to them on many levels if they are speaking the love language of physical touch. It shouts support, it shows that you are proud to be with them if you are holding hands in a public place, it shows love, and it tells them that you want them near you. Loaded, isn't it?

2. Try to give hugs that are as top class as your partner's. It may take some practice, but an unexpected snug little hug will melt their heart.

3. Then, there's the no-fail massage. In this case, you may just want to find out what kind of massage they like if they haven't thrown several hints in your direction previously. It's the perfect combination of sensuality and affection.

4. Tell your partner that you are listening when they are speaking by resting your hand lightly on their arm in a conversation.

5. Put your arm around your partner's shoulder and draw them close to you when you feel there's a notable distance between the two of you.

It's important to know that, if you have a partner whose primary love language is physical touch, and you're experiencing intimacy issues, it may be because these basic acts of physical affection are missing in your day-to-day interaction. These physical interactions set the foundation for a strong sexual bond and a healthy sex life, specifically if one or both partners speak the native tongue of physical touch. This love language also needs to be approached creatively if you and your partner are going to be spending an extended period of time apart. In a case like this, no one can blame anyone for not touching someone simply because it's not possible. However, proper communication can help ease the pain and do something small like leaving your partner a shirt you wore that smells like you or chatting on Skype or Zoom. If you're into it, you can even play games online. You'll find your way, as long as you know the basics, you know your partner, and you know where you want the relationship to go (Benniger, 2020).

This Is What You Shouldn't Do

There are three things that are very important when it comes to the love languages and understanding how they work. You should be familiar with all of them and not only the ones that are applicable to your relationships or situation. Then, you need to know your own love language and you also need to know your partner's. The reason why it's important to be familiar with all the love languages is that most of us have a little of all of them in us. We'll most likely have a primary one that comes out on top, but the others won't be nonexistent; we are multifaceted creatures. This also means that there may be mutual points when it comes to your love languages and the ones your partner has. For example, you may both be the same percentage "acts of service," which can develop into a point of mutual understanding when it comes to your needs.

A common mistake many couples make is to think that learning about the love languages is not going to result in a teamwork effort. In most cases, it does because there is always room for improvement, even if one side requires more improvement than the other. Even if the biggest issue lies with one partner, the ultimate display of love and partnership is making a team effort out of understanding and mastering each other's love languages. Always keep in mind that what you are doing is applying a general idea to an individual human being, so you need to be on the lookout for reactions, outcomes, and situations that can give you valuable feedback for your decision-making process going forward.

It's very helpful to know if your partner has more than one love language, especially if they are kind of evenly spread out instead of one language standing out tall above the rest. Knowing that your partner is, for example, 34% physical touch, 22% acts of services, 5% receiving gifts, and 39% quality time, I know that there are actually two competing needs with two less significant ones lurking in the background. In a case like this, you can ask your partner if they have a preference, or you can be a creative genius and do both. Either way, don't assume that your partner's primary love language is the only one.

Chapter 4:

Stop Throwing Things!

Has your partner ever thrown something? Even worse, have they ever thrown something at you? My partner threw a hotdog bun at me once. A dry, stale, hotdog bun. Not even a hint of ketchup, mustard, or butter, and no hotdog in sight. We were in the middle of a heated argument, and I mustered my ultimate comeback. I first sniggered and then asked, "Can you at least make an effort and throw something at me that will have the desired effect?!" My suggestion being that if he wanted to hurt or kill me by throwing something at me, he would need something heavier than a hotdog bun. He understood my reference and it made him livid, of course. We both knew that no-one wanted to hurt anyone, but the back-and-forth rose out of control and to the point where we were throwing things and doing the exact opposite of constructively working through our problems. During the time that this happened, we were both nineteen years old and I must say, more than a decade-and-a-half later, things can still spin out of control if you don't check what comes out of your mouth, or your hands, for that matter. However, nothing has been thrown back and forth but words since that incident. So, why do partners fight? With this, I mean what is the underlying source of the conflict—the emotional trigger that causes anger, irritation, and resentment? Let's explore this important component on how to build and maintain a healthy marriage and partnership.

Jealousy

I think we all get it. Sometimes, it's really hard not to be jealous. If you've been with a few people in your lifetime, you've probably come across someone who self-identifies as the "jealous type." When is jealousy unhealthy in a relationship, and how can you identify when destructive behavior stems from jealousy? First, it's important to understand healthy and unhealthy jealousy so one can distinguish between the two. You also wouldn't want to have a partner who doesn't feel the tiniest pang of jealousy when they see you with someone else, even if you are in an open relationship? It means that they are into you. The important part is how partners handle it under the circumstances of their relationship.

If you are overly jealous in your relationship, you are limiting your partner's ability to be independent and inhibiting their feeling of freedom. In many cases, it is a person's sense of independence that attracts a partner, and jealousy indicates that an individual is more needy than independent. If this is the case, your partner can lose their sense of attraction and the reason they were interested in you in the first place. But wait, that's not all! The jealous partner may not understand why the affected partner has changed and seems less interested or trying to break free, which can lead to more resentment and complicated emotions. Talk about a chain reaction.

Jealousy doesn't only affect your partner; it also affects your health. For example, it causes excessive stress that originates from what would mostly be unrealistic fears and scenarios created in the mind. If you are the extreme jealous type, you can even expect to develop health problems such as high blood pressure, ulcers, back pain, and if you want to go all out, you can end up with a heart attack and, I suspect, the absence of a partner. Also, don't forget your mental wellbeing. Jealousy cannot be good for mental health because it creates the need to control others, self-doubt, and possible paranoia. Jealous types are prone to misinterpret or misconceive situations that would otherwise be interpreted as normal and take them out of proportion. This is because someone who is jealous on a toxic level perceives the world around them through this distorted lens, which can lead to mental instability (Collins & Collins, 2020).

Other ways jealousy can damage a relationship is by making even small and everyday things difficult, like talking about everyday topics without having a fight. It increases the likelihood that an argument that has previously been regarded as dealt with will be brought up again unnecessarily, and eventually, your partner may question the reason why they are still in the relationship due to the constant conflict and lack of trust (Collins & Collins, 2020). Can you blame such a person for assessing the situation and weighing their happiness against staying in a toxic relationship? Jealousy stems from a heightened sense of insecurity, so if you know that this is an obstacle in your life and that it's affecting your relationship, it's time to face this demon.

Look at the way you are behaving toward your partner. Do they behave in the same way towards you? For example, if you decide to go out with friends, do they constantly text you or call you, asking when you're coming home? When you get home, would they be upset that you've been out for too long and express disbelief about where you were? If your partner is bringing up concerns of jealous behavior, try to avoid anger to be your first reaction. Instead, do introspection and look closely at your behavior. It can be helpful if your partner can provide examples of jealous behavior. The hard part is to look at these examples objectively and from your partner's perspective. If you only use your own perspective, you may not be able to identify any issues. You need to do this because it is important to understand why your partner feels this way. Are you blowing up small situations that should be regarded as non-issues? Also, are you being reasonable and giving your partner enough freedom? If your partner is the type of person who requires a lot of freedom and this makes you feel threatened, you may need to discuss it with them.

The most effective way to understand your own jealous tendencies is to search for the root of the issue. For example, can you identify any insecurities or are you being threatened in any way that warrants a defensive reaction? If the individual is only feeling emotionally threatened and there is an absence of any realistic threat, then they need to explore why they experience these emotions and how they can work with their partner to gain emotional confidence. Keep in mind that jealousy is a form of reactive behavior, although a complex one that is difficult to control. Understanding the issue is the first step towards improving and fixing (PsychAlive, 2010).

Insecurities

People's insecurities have so many different origins and are as diverse as the earth's insect population. There are common insecurities that many people share, but then there are also insecurities people have about the things that make them unique. May it be a lazy eye, buckteeth, a birthmark between their toes or bum cheeks, or even a shrill cackle reminiscent of an old horror movie. These insecurities may exist because others made them feel like their traits are not normal and would ridicule them for it. Not all people respond well to this kind of treatment, and some can develop psychological issues that will affect relationships they may have in the future. The more intimate the relationship, the more this issue may come into play.

The era we live in boasts a perception of beauty and social status that is practically unattainable without artificial means. This environment does not help the situation and can create feelings of anxiety and insecurity when you liken yourself to such unrealistic images. Insecurities are accompanied by an inner dialogue called the "critical inner voice." This inner voice is formed and cultivated by painful past experiences that often come from critical parents, teachers, or peers. Additionally, insecurities can develop just by being influenced by someone's attitude, so it doesn't necessarily need the impact of words or other gestures (PsychAlive, 2015). These experiences you have growing up and even in adulthood can cause you to ask questions like, "Why would anyone ever be interested in me?"

Feeling insecure every now and then is normal, but if there are deeply-rooted insecurities that you struggle with and that affect your relationship, you may need to go back to your self esteem's drawing board. Let's look at a few examples of how someone may experience insecurities in a relationship as a starting point. First, are you constantly worried that your partner is going to leave you or that they are planning on leaving you? Do you also feel that you don't really have anything to offer in the relationship and you keep going back to instances in your relationship to dwell on mistakes you made? Insecurities like feeling dumb, overweight, or boring are also an indication as this means you are not comfortable in your own skin within the relationship. Finally, do you often pressure your partner for reassurance and compliments but then not believing them or experiencing them as genuine? For example, "you're only saying that to make me feel better" or "you don't really believe that." Does that sound like you?

One of the most important elements that make a relationship successful is that the bond between partners is authentic and unique. In order to have such an authentic connection with your partner, you need to be able to open up, show your vulnerable side, and allow yourself to be loved. Deep insecurities prevent this from happening, which means the relationship cannot fully blossom and develop into a healthy state. Insecurities can prevent you from exposing your true self to your partner, which prevents the authentic connection between you (Admin, 2020). Even if you don't have any serious insecurity issues, exposing yourself to someone else is not easy. We're talking about true intimacy here and reaching this point can take time while you build trust in your relationship.

Chronic insecurities in a relationship can cause you or your partner to worry constantly about things that the other is probably not aware of or doesn't see as an issue. Excessive worrying is damaging for one's emotional wellbeing. Additionally, if one's habit of worrying elevates to the point that it manifests and causes irrational behavior, the relationship can suffer serious damage. An example of this is acting out based on jealousy as we discussed earlier. However, insecurities can manifest as other behavioral traits that can cause a relationship to suffer, such as chronic negativity. Perpetual negativity from your partner will cause emotional exhaustion and it may even cause you to start feeling insecure for no reason. Why should someone feel insecure because someone else is projecting their insecurities? Before this relationship problem starts to snowball, here's what you can do to identify and deal with nagging insecurities.

It is crucial that you identify where your insecurities come from. As we mentioned, many insecurities come from past experiences, and a lot of them develop due to communication issues between children and their perceived idols or guardians. My grandmother never praised or acknowledged her children when they achieved something. Instead, she would use the opportunity to tell them that they can improve without providing reassurance or praise or she would criticize their achievements. Her children all became very successful individuals in different fields that range from law to the arts, but I grew up observing my talented mother's crippling self-doubt and insecurities. This affected her relationships—all of them. It's like observing someone trapped in a bubble of self-perception, but you can't break through and help them change their perception or realize their own potential. I once made the mistake of telling my grandmother I got an A for an exam, and her reaction was, "It could've been a perfect score." If you've never understood how deep insecurities can go and from how far back in your life they can come, maybe this can be a helpful indication.

However deep these insecurities may run through your being, it's not healthy to hold onto them. The first piece of advice would be to give yourself a break. Don't allow that inner voice to be so critical. People who are insecure sometimes don't realize that they have probably received more positive feedback and compliments from people than bad ones, but because the bad ones hurt so much, they didn't see any value in the good ones. If you have a very active inner critic, you may want to counter its irritating voice with some self-affirmations. Self-affirmations may be hard to do at first because you feel silly repeating positive beliefs about yourself to yourself. It can even feel like you're faking it. Well, that's where the "fake it 'til you make it" comes in. Because you suffer from insecurities, and they may be deeply ingrained in you, your affirmations will feel superficial at first. But give them time to grow on you. Choose qualities that you know are your strengths, but you also know that you don't really allow yourself to acknowledge them. Open that door for yourself. Each time you practice inspiring and complimenting yourself, it'll become easier and you'll start seeing the truth in these affirmations. Positivity is contagious, and your partner will experience a renewed appreciation for qualities they probably admired and found attractive from the start.

Furthermore, if you've set any conditions for yourself in the past that you needed to achieve or adhere to in order to deserve love, let them go. That familiar voice in your head that told you someone will only love you under these or those conditions needs to hit the road. Accepting yourself is the key to others accepting you. Be compassionate when dealing with your insecurities and remember that your partner chose you because of the qualities you have.

Finally, the most productive way to deal with insecurities without them affecting your relationship negatively is by being open and honest with your partner. Tell them about your struggles and express your willingness to confront your insecurities. This, in itself, is a strength and something to be proud of, and your partner will most likely respect you even more for this. By communicating openly with your partner, you can also give them a chance to help you deal with these issues by not only alerting your partner about them but also giving your partner the chance to act mindfully in this regard. Try to meet each other halfway and take a leap in the name of love. By consistently affirming your strong points, letting go of your restrictive conditions, and creating a space that encourages open communication, you can open up this liberating and exciting new avenue in your relationship (Admin, 2020).

Pride

Is pride really such a deadly sin? In relationships, that seems to be the case. If not deadly, it certainly doesn't seem to be very popular or productive. Prideful behavior includes a sense of superiority towards one's partner that comes down to a sense of entitlement when it comes to how they are allowed to feel and act. This comes down to a lack of humility, which is a crucial quality required from both partners in a healthy relationship. You'll know your partner suffers from the pride delusion if they never want to admit that they're wrong or always want to win an argument (which, to them, is about winning and losing), and the effect it has on their partner doesn't seem to bother them at all. Basically, there is a total lack of respect, and the funny thing is that you may notice them acting more respectful towards others than they do towards you.

When being confronted or challenged during an altercation, their classic move is to flip the issue around and onto their partner or "opponent." This behavior is the opposite of productive because, instead of doing introspection and showing recognition for their partner's feelings and opinions, they immediately position themselves reactively by going on the defensive. If your partner does not feel the need to set boundaries regarding their behavior towards you, then this should also be a warning sign. A prideful partner's reactions and behavior is likened to the "fight or flee" response associated with fear or a crisis situation. The saddest and most ironic part of this is that such an individual will only experience true freedom in a relationship once they let go of their controlling and egotistical behavior.

The first, and I suspect the hardest, step is acknowledging that you are a prideful person because this will also mean that your destructive behavior has likely led to the deterioration or the ending of relationships. However, it is not too late. There is still hope; all it takes is a first step of willingness. If you can start by setting your pride aside to explore the cause and origin of this behavior, you have already taken a giant step in the right direction. It is not easy for a prideful person to spend time examining their own issues because that's what they are running from. If you can show your partner that you are capable of being vulnerable and receptive, they will also be willing to support you in this transformational process. Another personal challenge you can take on is to be humble in situations where your pride would normally get the best of you. True humility is liberating because you start to realize that egotistical behavior only controls one person, and that's you. Humility is about acknowledging the importance of others' feelings, especially your partner's, valuing their opinion, and seeing yourself as their equal. This is a true mind shift that will make you mentally strong and bring happiness to you and those around you. Finally, allow yourself recognition for the positive changes you've made and acknowledge the improvement they've made on your partner's life and your relationship. Even if there are obstacles ahead, staying on course and seeing the positive effects it has on you and your relationship will make it all worthwhile. Make this a personal goal for self-improvement that will transform your relationship with your partner (Gunther, 2020).

Even the most prideful individuals will experience a time in their life when they can't rely on their pride to get them through things. We all need our partners at one point or another to rely on and for support. This type of situation should be like a flash of light in a dark room to them—to see that it does not take away any of their self-worth when they need the help of others. Additionally, one can learn how rewarding it can be to allow those who love you, like your partner, to support you.

Hormones (Yes, Hormones)

Some of the first changes in your body when you fall in love with someone are all linked to hormones. As your relationship progresses and starts to develop its unique niches and quirks, hormones can come into play again and cause possible conflict and misunderstandings. These misunderstandings, however, are likely linked to different hormones than the ones that raged through your veins at the beginning of your relationship, and a possible imbalance can occur from time-to-time. We're way past the point where someone can get away with saying, "Oh, I see it's PMS o'clock again" when you're feeling a bit under the weather, but it's still important to be educated about how hormones can affect us mentally across the entire gender spectrum.

Traditionally, hormonal issues that cause mood changes are associated with women because they don't only have more major role-playing hormones than men, but these hormones are incredibly powerful. While we normally regard testosterone as a male hormone, females also have testosterone, along with progesterone and estrogen. However, the hormones that influence us the most at the start of a relationship are oxytocin and dopamine. Oxytocin is known as the "love hormone" for several reasons. One reason is because it has been detected at higher levels in individuals who are experiencing the feeling of being "in love" or who are in the initial stages of a romantic relationship than in individuals who are not experiencing these feelings. But this neural Cupid is also known to have an influence on sexual interaction, including the intensity of orgasms, and it can enhance important aspects of relationships, including positive memories and communication, trust, fidelity, and bonding (Santos-Longhurst & Pelley, 2018).

Oxytocin also works in tandem with dopamine and serotonin, which are also known as the "happy hormones," so when it's secreted in that honeymoon phase of your relationship, it makes you feel like you're on cloud nine.

There are, however, other hormones that can affect a relationship due to how it affects a partner, and more often than not, these hormones cause confusion and frustration—likely because their role has not been identified yet or their effects are misunderstood or underestimated. Current studies have shown that normal female hormone fluctuations can affect not only the owner of these hormones but also their partner's judgement and welfare. The role hormones play in our well-being and everyday functioning are often dismissed, underestimated, or downplayed. These studies are based on women who were not using any form of contraception, as any contraceptive device changes hormonal functioning. The studies were also conducted on heterosexual couples so that the interplay between the female and male hormones, which are so vastly different, can be observed. One of the observations indicated that when a woman's estradiol or estrogen levels are high, their partner regards them to be less satisfied in the relationship, so consequently, they felt less satisfied. It's almost like a chain reaction. The conclusion, however, was that normal fluctuations of hormones are not likely to cause serious issues in a relationship as only small fluctuations were observed. To conclude, healthy hormonal fluctuations are not going to ruin a good relationship, and it's definitely not going to save a sinking one (Dolan, 2020).

Now that we know this, we have to look at instances where there are hormonal imbalances. This can include a condition like menopause and should not be regarded as a "fault" of the individual who has to deal with the imbalance. I don't think anyone can deny that menopause has the potential to wreak havoc in a relationship due to the female body undergoing a complete transformation. I remember a comedian once unapologetically describing it as leaving the summer season of fertility and entering the dry and cold winter of old age. If you think about it that way, even though it is very harshly put, one should offer nothing but support for someone who is going through menopause. However, let's start afresh. Let's throw all generalizations of menopause out the window, including our comedian's take on it. We all know the sketch of the moody, irritated, and angry partner that suddenly breaks out in a sweat due to regular hot flushes. Let's ignore this and regard menopause as a process each woman goes through as an individual. The symptoms may be similar, but women are individuals. Factual evidence indicates that women who undergo the menopausal process experience a heightened sense of anxiety, stress, and can even experience depression. These symptoms can put a strain on the relationship, so it is important for both partners to move away from the stereotype and understand what is taking place in their situation from an individual perspective. For example, if your partner is already prone to anxiety, this is something that should receive extra attention, and would not necessarily be a problem in another relationship. It is also possible that someone who is experiencing menopausal symptoms are also dealing with insecurities because it is also seen as a symbol of transition. These complicated emotions may cause them to feel insecure in their relationship and isolated from their partner.

In a situation like this where hormones can cause misunderstandings between partners and may even cause them to drift apart due to a lack of communication, there are a few important things both partners can do to stay connected and supportive. If you are going through this hormonal process or through any other hormonal imbalance, it's important to still practice self-care. This will not only help you to feel better but will also help you to achieve a sense of control. Self-care in this case focuses on your mental and physical health. So, if you can, consult your doctor for advice on hormonal supplements or a complimentary diet that may alleviate some of the worst symptoms. If you are on the other end of such a relationship, you can provide support and show that you care by not only trying to be less reactive when you see your partner overreacting or being moody, but also to provide an ear and a shoulder of comfort. During this process, you, as a couple, can work on solving the physical cause of the relationship issues because, luckily, you know that the cause is physiological and temporary ("Are Your Hormones Ruining Your Relationship?" 2018). This hopefully also counts for other hormonal issues that influence your relationship with your partner. It comes down to openness, clear avenues of communication, and an act or two of selflessness.

Those Choices

When it comes to the conflict situation itself, there are ways you can fight fairly instead of fighting dirty. If you love each other and you are dedicated to making the relationship the best it can possibly be, then of course you would want conflict to be healthy. There are couples who never fight. They also most likely never laugh together, hold hands, or say things like, "I love you." This is not how I'm suggesting your relationship should be like. Keep in mind that it's healthy to fight because it brings the issue at hand out in the open. The problem is that conflict often occurs spontaneously, which means that both parties react based on emotion instead of taking a step back and looking at the situation rationally. The following pointers are directly linked to the discussion of healthy communication in the first chapter, but they are specifically aimed at diffusing a conflict situation and helping partners sort out conflict in a productive way.

If you want to sort out a situation, you shouldn't be afraid of conflict. What I mean is that, if conducted constructively, conflict is not a bad thing, so it shouldn't be feared or viewed in a negative light. See conflict as an opportunity for your relationship to grow. You can bet that you and your partner are going to disagree on some things; even more so because your relationship is on such an intimate level. Some couples fight more than others, but it doesn't mean that there's less love. If you and your partner can talk about approaching conflict constructively, then there's no reason to fear a conflict situation. It can even be satisfying.

One of the things I think we've all been guilty of when fighting is attacking the person and not the issue. This happens during conflict because you feel personally attacked, so you want to retaliate by going full-throttle *ad hominem* on your partner. This is a very destructive habit and it comes directly from experiencing a primary emotional reaction. It's important for both partners to make a mind-switch here to keep the conflict situation healthy. If your partner is trying to be rational, don't become even more triggered and see it as a personal attack. Focus on the issue instead of on each other. The issue is what needs sorting out. Be open and receptive, and keep your emotions to a minimum.

When you've managed to avoid having emotional reactions, you also need to stick to the main issue and not try to divert each other's attention to another issue. Stay with the current issue that caused the conflict situation. If one partner realizes that they are largely responsible for the issue, it's a natural reaction to change the focus to another issue that diverts the attention away from the primary problem. Don't do it! All you're doing is dragging out the fight and trying to delay solving the problem. If you play a part in the core issue, then your partner will respect you if you take responsibility for it so both of you can move forward. Also, if your fights start with frivolous topics like your partner leaving a dirty plate on their bedside table again, but like last time, the argument reverts back to a main theme like your partner drinking too much or the two of you not spending time together, this is a sign that you have not sorted out the main issue and that one of you is initiating conflict because the other is likely avoiding the main issue. In a situation like this, the main issue that you need to pay attention to and aim to resolve is the one you end up fighting about. If you deal with the main issue, the small nippy fights will go away.

When is an issue a legitimate issue between partners? Some people think an issue is only legitimate when both partners experience it as a problem. However, if this is the case, a partner who experiences an issue alone is going to remain dissatisfied and unhappy if the other partner refuses to acknowledge the issue. This is an example of where you need to understand that a relationship has two perspectives and two points of view. Even more importantly, one point of view is not more important than the other. Don't make the mistake of downplaying your partner's relationship concerns. If the issue affects your pride, for example, you should consider placing your relationship before your pride and show your partner that you are willing to work with them to solve the issue. Remember that a relationship where one partner gives 30% and the other gives 70% is eventually going to experience issues. Even in a 40%/60% case. Acknowledging each other's needs and opinions is an important part of this (Young, 2015).

Chapter 5:

Lessons Learned

Looking back at all my previous relationships, I can definitely see a pattern. I used to go for kooky, happy-go-lucky, blue-eyed boys that were always several years younger than me. You know, surfers, bird watchers without jobs, and guys that didn't know if they were coming or going. There's nothing wrong with that, but you can't be like that forever. I learned some priceless lessons from these relationships, like the fact that I needed to grow up and that I need to find someone who can give my tangled web of a life some structure. Surprisingly, that's exactly what happened. Somewhere, in the deepest depths of my mind, a shift occurred, and I ended up marrying a brown-eyed, responsible, older guy. I must add, though, he's just older by a few months. But character differences between guys I used to date and who I ended up marrying are like night and day. Take spontaneity as an example. I thrived on the "not having plans and just showing up everywhere with no money" lifestyle, but now I can't imagine living like that. I have to admit, it was stressful sometimes and it caused conflict in my relationships, so although I love a bit of spontaneity that I have to force out of my husband every now and then, being prepared and living a structured life makes me feel cared for because there's effort going into that. So, my main lesson from previous relationships is that I need structural support from a partner and, even though I crave that spontaneous and crazy life I used to live, I know that it comes with a lot of uncertainty. Now that I've delivered my overture, what about you? Let's look at some thoughts and ideas about learning from past relationships.

Common Lessons That People Learn

Some lessons one learns from relationships are inspiring and empowering, and others can be crushing, painful, and hard to accept. So, should you take them on the chin or carry them with you as baggage that will affect your next relationship?

Some of the things you can learn from failed relationships and breakups include your outlook on life, your perception of other people, how to communicate more effectively, how you can build your own strength and independence, and you also learn about the importance of balancing the give-and-take component. You can also learn all of these things when you are in a productive and healthy relationship, but there's something about a breakup that forces you to face the bare facts and puts you in a position where you need to decide whether you're going to learn from them or let them weigh you down. First, a breakup can teach you a lot about life and your perspective of it. In a romantic relationship, you become very close to your partner and usually both of you open up to a certain extent and show your strengths and vulnerabilities. If these qualities end up clashing to the point that the relationship needs to end, you've had the privilege of getting a glimpse of how life can be from someone else's perspective. What you do with this information is entirely up to you, but if you want to utilize it wisely, apply it to your own outlook by considering or even applying the good and discarding the bad. If you fought a lot, then you can use these differences to learn more about yourself, how you deal with difficult situations, how you deal with your emotions when they are at peak levels, and how you can handle this productively. It's all about being proactive in your approach because that will ultimately make your life easier and it will make you happier. If you've had unsuccessful relationships or breakups, there were most likely conflicts involved. How did you handle these conflict situations? Did you, for example, throw your ex with a dry hotdog bun? I hope not—you should at least add some mustard. If you have a fiery temper, have previous relationships helped you to tame the beast or have they only put more fuel on the fire? Most people learn something about their communication abilities after a failed relationship. Whether they implement these lessons to productively change their behavior if change is needed is unknown.

Communication in failed relationships can teach you more than just temper control and anger management. It can also help you to understand how to express yourself in different situations because, you know, sometimes one tends to think your partner is a mind reader. We have the capacity to sense what the other person is feeling, but to get the best results, express yourself. Expression leads to understanding. Mindful expression, which means that you assess the situation as well as your partner's state of mind before communicating, will ultimately improve your bond and bring you closer. The final point for communication in breakups is that it really teaches you how important effective communication is. You may not realize this after your first relationship because sometimes we tend to think the other person caused all the issues. Then, as you gain experience and you go out with someone who puts you in your place, you come to realize that communication is a two-way street. Some people are natural communicators and learn from the start, and others don't. But gaining experience in communication and learning from your mistakes are some of the upsides of otherwise unpleasant breakups.

If past relationships made you stronger and more open to experiencing different emotions, then you aced your test. This is a component that many people struggle with in relationships, and after a breakup, they tend to look back at uncomfortable emotional encounters as unpleasant memories instead of a learning opportunity. Emotional growth is different for everyone, but to enable yourself to have this opportunity, you need to be open to it. Another lesson that is available for most people to take and learn from in past relationships is that compatibility and chemistry are not always synonymous with one another. You may have ended a relationship because there was chemistry from the start, but eventually, both partners realized that the level of compatibility is not high enough. Compatibility relates to both partners having the same interests, beliefs, tastes, and possibly cultural background if it is important in the context of the relationship. On the other hand, when a couple is highly compatible but the chemistry levels are low, the relationship is likely to fizzle out due to a lack of passion. Breakups that occur due to an imbalance between compatibility and chemistry can teach you to look for that balance, and if you need to compromise on one of the two in a relationship because you want it to work, past experience will help you to navigate whether this is viable.

Finally, one of the most valuable lessons past relationships and breakups can teach us is when to let go. Have you ever been in a relationship that you know is past its expiration date, but yet you go through the daily motions as if nothing's wrong? Maybe we do this because we don't want to experience the conflict that occurs with a breakup or see our partners upset and cornered. Just because you want to break up with someone doesn't always mean you don't love them anymore. However, past relationships can teach you when you need to keep on fighting or when you need to let go. Even if this experience comes from being in relationships with other people, there will most likely be similar situations and circumstances that can lead you towards making the right decision. Also, if it's not about letting go of the relationship as a whole but about something that happened between you and your partner that you need to digest, the same experience can help you there. Learn when to hold on and when to let go (Seetubtim, 2014).

What Your Partner Needs to Know About Your Past

Your relationship choices say a lot about who you are, whether you've grown, and where you are headed in life. That said, you can learn a lot about yourself by looking at whether you tended to go for a specific type of partner in your past. If there's a pattern in the type of partner you used to date, then maybe you can learn something about yourself. So, how much of this should you divulge to the person you chose to spend the rest of your life with—even if they are an open-minded and accepting individual? Oversharing may damage your relationship, not because your partner will completely change their mind about you, but because it can plant the tiniest seed of doubt. We all go through different stages in life, and most of us change as we get older. If you have a raunchy past, what does your partner need to know about it? Except, that is, if they are part of it.

At the start of a relationship, you want to know everything about each other; not because you are suspicious, but because you are infatuated. You may feel that, in order to have a healthy relationship, your partner needs to know everything about your past, including past relationships. In this case, it may come down to assessing your partner as an individual, but also looking at general guidelines won't hurt, just to see what the mainstream consensus is in this matter. Relationship experts advise that it's best to always be cautious when it comes to revealing past information, especially if the information is about something you regret or find embarrassing. Consider the cons versus the pros, with an emphasis on the cons. Yes, this is one instance where it may be more productive if you take a pessimistic approach. Will anything bad happen if you don't tell your partner about the time you had that threesome in the backyard of the local church? Conversely, this may turn your partner on, so that's why you need to carefully examine the situation. The ideal measuring tool is the question, "Is this information crucial for the health of the relationship?" If it is, and it's the worst kind of awkward you've ever experienced, you may need to get your act together and spill the beans. But, if it's not, and you just wanted to tell your partner a very awkward story on a whim, think again. Why the sudden urge to share? Examine your need to divulge and if this need is productive or destructive. You're not obligated to share everything with your partner (Steber, 2018).

What would be considered information your partner needs to know about for the sake of the relationship? There is definitely some information that should be on a need-to-know basis. For example, if you are HIV positive or you've obtained an STD in a previous relationship, not telling your partner can seriously damage or even end the relationship. If you suffer from a chronic illness, this may not be as hard to tell your partner, but it is still important to do so. If you stay quiet about a condition that affects your quality of life, your partner may see this as a form of betrayal or assume that you don't trust them.

One or both of you may be the reserved type and not tell each other much about the other's past experiences or relationships. If your partner's silence is bothering you, try to keep an open mind as some individuals take longer to open up. However, if you've been married for a reasonable amount of time and you feel that there are reasonable details about your partner's life they do not want to share with you, it may be a good idea to try communicating openly and maintaining patience. The reason for this may stem from a myriad of reasons that can include a sense of insecurity, like the fact that your partner was sworn to secrecy by a family member or that, even though the information affects the health of the relationship, they are too embarrassed to tell you because it involves a decision they regret. Consider being married to someone who cannot have children due to having multiple abortions in the past. Now that she has met you, she would want to have children, but her past choices affected her body in such a way that this is not possible anymore. In that point in her life, having an abortion was her best option. This can be an incredibly painful thing to tell your partner—that you have to deny them something like having children because of choices you had to make in the past in order to survive. It's always good to go back to that communication manual. It's applicable on all major bases of intimate relationship.

What are the most commonly-asked questions between couples that can make them squirm and a bit uncomfortable? They are mostly about sex, of course. Here's an overview of the most cringy ones and how you could approach them when confronted.

The first one that's on all of our minds is the "So, how many people have you been with?" question. I would evaluate this question in my head by asking "So, what kind of partner are you?" What I mean with this question is, is your partner the jealous type? Are they open and liberal or more conservative? What is the actual reason why they are asking you this question? Usually, partners want to know this because they want to use it as a way to evaluate you. However, your sexual past may not have anything to do with who you are now. So, with this question, I'd say providing the information is not necessary except if you have a good reason for telling your partner. Use your own discretion (Gordon, 2019).

Another interesting question that you may encounter is your partner asking you about how many times you've seriously been in love (Gordon, 2019). This question kind of gives off warning signals because of the likely reasons someone would ask you this. The most likely reason would stem from a sense of insecurity as your partner may be trying to figure out if you've loved someone more than you love them now. I'd suggest giving them a reassuring answer without providing too many details about this particular topic. For example, you can help them to understand that there's a reason why you are married to them and not involved in any of your previous relationships anymore. A similar situation would be if your partner is particularly interested in previous breakups and why your previous relationships didn't last. While you may have learned from these experiences, which is something your partner may not know, they may be trying to look for possible issues or use the information to profile you in a way. This behavior does not mean that your partner doesn't trust you. I can be a subconscious defense mechanism. Keeping this in mind, make sure that you assess the situation and don't feel obliged to tell your partner every detail about your past.

The final question you should think twice about before giving a straight answer is how good your previous partners were in bed or what your experience was like having sex with them (Gordon, 2019). Telling your partner about intimate details from previous relationships is most likely going to upset them and may be the source of your partner developing insecurities sexually. You do get partners who are turned on by these kinds of details, but make sure to observe your partner closely so you can try and identify the reason for their curiosity.

Learn From It

There are ways you can see whether you've learned from your past relationships and whether past struggles, heartbreak, and conflict is holding you back. Sometimes, you are not capable of seeing this because we humans are naturally subjective. In order to recognize issues and conduct true introspective processing, one must make a mental shift towards being objective, which can sometimes mean staring your own flaws in the face. The past will always have an impact on our lives, but it is how you choose to deal with the past and use it that makes the difference.

In romantic relationships, partners sometimes subconsciously repeat previous behaviors in an attempt to make up for mistakes they think they made in previous relationships. This behavioral trait is called repetition compulsion, and an individual who has this compulsion follows a path that leads to a dead end by pursuing similar partners and using similar behaviors to try and fix past mistakes and failed relationships. These compulsions can even develop and be influenced by relationships you experienced as a child, even if these early relationships were not romantically-oriented.

Luckily, there are ways you can identify repetitive compulsive traits in your current relationship, so it's not too late to end the pattern. One of the ways you can identify this trait is if you are always attracted to the same type of person, especially if they are narcissistic or have other destructive habits. What this means is that you need to deal with how the person who caused you sadness and hurt when you were young affects you in the present, as your behavior indicates that you have not yet worked through the pain. If you are especially prone to experience empathy towards others, you may find yourself attracted to more toxic personalities because of your basic desire to fix them. If you can identify such a pattern and you are currently experiencing relationship difficulties, you may want to consult a therapist to see if you need to deal with any painful experiences you had in the past that can possibly be influencing your relationships (Dodgson, 2018).

Another indicator that you are carrying emotional baggage that doesn't stretch as far back is something therapists call "tainted pleasures." These are things you may have enjoyed doing with previous partners, but now that you are in your current relationship, these activities somehow make you feel angry or even guilty. This is an indication that there is unfinished business that you need to deal with as bringing these feelings into your current relationship or marriage is unfair towards your partner. Such an activity can be from traumatizing to infuriating to leaving you with unbearable feelings of guilt. If this is a phase you are going through and you know that it's beginning to fade, then that is a normal part of healing after a breakup, but if you are now married to someone else or in a new long-term relationship and you are still experiencing these feelings, you have an unhealthy attachment to your previous relationship. Keep in mind that a tainted pleasure can be something as simple as a song, a place, or a movie (Dodgson, 2018).

If you know that you have sexually-related hang ups that link back to previous relationships, this is an issue that you need to sort out urgently. If your partner came into the relationship with no physical or sexual hangups linked to their previous partner, you need to honor this and do the same. For example, you don't like a certain sex position because it reminds you of your ex, you are still influenced by the way your ex viewed you sexually, or there are specific ways you don't like to be touched because of your previous partner. If these reasons generally make you uncomfortable, then it's an entirely different situation, but if you can sense that your ex is still in the picture when you feel that sense of discomfort, you need to talk to someone about it. Try talking to a therapist first before talking to your partner directly; you may be able to sort out the issue without having to expose your partner to the situation.

Communication is something that we discussed at length earlier. We also discussed the inability to communicate, obstacles that affect communication, and how it can affect a relationship. So, one thing you need to establish when you are experiencing these communication issues from your side is whether the source of the issue involves past relationship experiences. This is fairly common because of how integral communication is in a relationship and how ineffective communication from an intimate partner can affect us. For example, if you had a partner that you thought never took you seriously or never really listened to you, chances are that you may be projecting this frustration on your current partner by communicating more aggressively when it is not required. If you identify that your communication methods are compulsive and emotional, this may be the first sign that you are reacting to previous and possibly frustrating experiences. This kind of thing happens without a person even realizing it, and there are more people guilty of this kind of projection than you think. It's always good to trace back your steps and look for the source of the problem.

If you come from one or even a string of abusive relationships, you likely have a diminished sense of respect for yourself. This, again, can be caused by other factors, but if you can clearly identify this pattern in previous relationships, that's how you're going to start learning from it. Disrespect manifests in behavior like telling yourself off, insulting yourself, telling yourself you're stupid or ugly, or scolding yourself for small mistakes. What you need to realize is that this is not actually you talking to yourself but your previous partners' hurtful comments you are projecting on yourself. If you are able to realize this, it's a giant step in the right direction. However, it's still going to hurt while you process the feelings you compressed. Give yourself a chance to deal with this old baggage if your current partner is supportive and loving. Don't let these hurtful comments keep on echoing in your mind.

Have you ever recreated unpleasant situations from past relationships in your mind and experienced them like they were almost really happening? This is a clear indication that your relationship history has not been erased from your mental browser and it is popping up again even though it may not be relevant anymore. What you are actually doing when reliving situations from past relationships is not living in the present moment with your partner, and you deny yourself and your partner the opportunity to create new and precious memories. This tendency to compulsively think back to things that hurt or upset you is not a conscious choice you make, but you need to deal with the cause of this habit to ensure your current relationship has a chance to develop and bloom. Don't underestimate the power of your mind and how these memories and your emotional connection can affect your current relationship. You can try visualization exercises in which your thoughts are about a specific person. For example, if this individual appears large and menacing in your mind, force your perception of them to become smaller and smaller every time you experience those thoughts, until they are miniscule and you can squish them between your finger and thumb. Think in terms of proactivity. A reactive mind would allow non-related issues to influence and contaminate a relationship that shows potential (Dodgson, 2018).

If you are going through your relationship with constant doubt in your mind and you find it necessary to look over your shoulder often, this means that there are issues from part relationships you haven't dealt with. This is, of course, if you've never experienced any indication that your current partner is cheating on you. Doubts and trust issues are formed in previous relationships and you carry them over into a new relationship, except if your current partner has given you a reason to think that they are not trustworthy. This, however, does not include any paranoid thoughts or suspicions. If you are experiencing these feelings of doubt and you haven't encountered any reason to distrust your current partner, it's time to revisit previous relationships and see if you can identify a cause that led to a pattern of automatic distrust (Dodgson, 2018). If your partner has noticed this behavior, it's best to open up to them about it and help them to understand that they are not the source of the problem. You need to do more than communicate with them, though. It's important to work through these troubling feelings, and if you have a partner that is supportive and loving, they can help you with the process. If you want to involve your partner in your healing process, then communicating the problem in a clear and mindful way is the best way to gain their trust and acceptance.

Chapter 6:

The (In)Famous Apology

Not only is there a lot of written information about the apology, but everyone also has their own opinion about apologies in relationships, and some people even have a lot to say while they're apologizing—almost like they want to unload emotionally and bring up the whole issue again instead of offering a sincere apology! Whichever way, looking at the apology from different angles will provide you with insight about its value and meaning in a relationship, why it's important, and also when you should and shouldn't apologize. Some partners apologize for everything while others refuse to apologize for anything. Research has indicated that the most prominent reasons individuals don't apologize include the fact that they don't actually care about their partner as much as they think they do or they aren't concerned about their partner, they don't like apologizing because it has a negative effect on their self-image, or they just don't believe that an apology is going to make any difference. This, nevertheless, does not provide any reputable reason why apologies cannot be constructive in some cases. What do you need to know about when and how to apologize? There are some definite ground rules that have been carved out of generations of related disputes.

What Apologizing Can Do for Your Relationship

The most difficult thing about apologies in a relationship can be when partners don't agree or see eye to eye about how and when to apologize. In cases like these, it's important to take a step back and look at how important apologizing is. Take a moment to pause and realize that it's not about getting your way regarding how and when you apologize, but more about reaching a consensus that makes both partners feel appreciated and respected—what an apology is supposed to do. Apologizing makes some people feel weak and vulnerable, which may be something they fear greatly, while others may feel that they do everything wrong and apologize constantly. Both approaches are wrong and can damage relationships, as they are not healthy approaches that will lead to a healthy or balanced outcome.

One of the most important qualities that an apology should have is sincerity, which means that it should not be forced, and the individual has to really mean what they are saying. True sincerity has several benefits that can repair and strengthen a relationship after a fight or after someone made a mistake. When you apologize sincerely, you are telling your partner that you understand what you did wrong, how it affected them, and that you understand the relationship's parameters and rules. A sincere apology allows your partner to feel safe and reassured about your actions as they can sense that you are truly sorry for what you've done. Sincere apologies, especially if you've hurt your partner's feelings or embarrassed them, can re-establish their sense of dignity and repair their sense of self-worth. This may be an obvious one, but it's worth repeating: a sincere apology has the ability to effectively clear any uncomfortable feelings and opens up a door for conversation and discussion that is necessary for healing. This component is what makes sincere apologies so hard for some individuals. Sincere apologies clearly indicate your admittance of guilt or wrongdoing. However, if you fit this description, keep in mind that, simultaneously, a sincere apology also shows character and your willingness to build and work on your relationship with your partner, which is extremely important for healthy relationships. Apologizing effectively can ultimately relieve a lot of stress from your relationship and prevent a future conflict that would have occurred had you been reactive instead of sincere, which, in this case, is a good example of proactive behavior. Here are some productive ideas that can help you to understand the sincere apology.

- Understand the different reasons why one should apologize. Because there are reasons that support apologies and reasons that support not apologizing, knowing the difference can help you understand your fault and subsequently bring out your sincere side. Reasons include showing your partner that you understand your mistake, opening up a discussion about the relationship rules, and learning from your mistakes.
- Sincerity is also linked to timing. For example, would you regard an apology from your partner for cheating on you while they are in the loo as sincere? Shouting it through the open door? The crassness of this example removes any doubt in my mind that you, now, still don't understand the link between sincerity and timing. However, let's counter it with a nicer example anyway. Depending on what you're apologizing about, you may want to show your partner that you are taking the situation seriously by sitting next to them, holding their hand, making them a cup of tea, and making direct eye contact with them while you make your apology. None of these are included in the example above. Make sure that the moment is right. If your partner is really angry and there is no right moment, just make a heartfelt and sincere apology while making sure your body is facing theirs directly if possible, to indicate your undivided attention.
- A sincere apology includes a true expression of regret for what you have done. Regret is also a clear indication that you understand what you've done and why it was wrong or hurtful towards your partner. Express your regret by saying something like "I wish I thought it through before I acted and hurt your feelings." By talking in retrospect while expressing your regret, you will show your partner that you are able to identify what hurt them and that you have remorse for your actions.
- Sincerity is a great tool you can use to make amends. If you can get a solid start on making amends directly after you've

apologized, you're more than halfway there. Keep your eyes open for any signs from your partner that they are ready to have a healing conversation. If you broke their trust, make an effort to see what you can do to work on your trust relationship to rebuild it. Communication is key here.

- Another function and purpose of a sincere apology are for both partners to reaffirm the relationship boundaries. One of you has overstepped a boundary that you were or were not aware of prior to the incident, so what better time than this to make sure that you are both on the same page? Reaffirming boundaries is not always a simple process with both parties agreeing on everything but working on this aspect of your relationship ensures less future misunderstandings and mishaps. Healthy boundaries are a fundamental component of a healthy relationship.

- An apology is not sincere if you are not apologizing for the right reason. Only apologize if there is a reason to do so, otherwise, it is impossible to be sincere.

- Your sincerity should stretch as far as you were in the wrong; a sincere apology does not translate into apologizing on your partner's behalf. It should focus solely on the part you have to own up to and nothing more. This final point is directly connected to our next discussion point, which is when is an apology a good idea and when is it a bad idea? There are several contributing factors to consider.

Good Idea Versus Bad Idea

Apologizing, however, even sincerely, is not always a good idea. A basic guideline that can come in handy to measure when an apology is a good idea is the following: If you have done something that has caused your partner pain, whether intentionally or unintentionally, an apology is a good idea. For example, if you said something that your partner found hurtful, but you didn't know that your partner would feel this way about this specific opinion, it is still a good idea to offer a sincere apology; not because you are the weaker one but because your apology will provide comfort and a sense of safety for your partner which will allow you to discuss the situation openly and honestly. If you did it on purpose, then there's no question about it—you need to apologize and then some. If you did something wrong on purpose, apologizing is going to be a lot harder because you're going to have to do some introspection about why you wanted to hurt your partner. Do you want to share those feelings with them? For example, did you do it on purpose because of jealousy or another strong emotion your partner invoked in you? If this deeper issue that caused you to hurt your partner has not been addressed yet, will you be able to offer a sincere apology? In this case, even though you may have an issue that made you act the way you did, there is still a reason for a sincere apology. Keep in mind that hurting your partner is not a productive way to deal with your feelings, especially if your partner is not aware of them. If you look at the situation from this perspective, then apologizing for approaching the situation in the wrong way and thereby hurting your partner unnecessarily warrants a sincere apology. This doesn't mean that you are apologizing for the way your partner made you feel; however, your apology about your incorrect approach can serve as the ideal platform to discuss this issue with your partner. All that this means is that you are taking responsibility for hurting your partner and you are also proactively creating a platform for a further productive discussion.

So, when is apologizing a bad idea? Is it possible? Oh yes, it is. If you are not planning on offering a sincere apology, don't apologize. It's going to make things worse, whether you did something 'small' or something 'big.' Your partner may see the small thing as a big thing and you can hurt them even more if you disregard their point of view and offer a la-di-dah apology. An insincere apology is going to close any possible door or portal that could've opened up for further healing and discussion and place a lock on it.

Bad apologies or situations where apologies are not going to suffice are often based on bad, spur-of-the-moment decisions like making promises you know you won't be able to stick to. Another example is if you're just lying for the sake of satisfying your partner for a while, like promising to change your behavior until they catch you doing what you promised not to do again.

Apologizing is also not a good idea if you did nothing wrong or, as we mentioned earlier, if you are not apologizing for your own mistakes. Sometimes, this situation depends on perspective, but if you know your partner well, especially after spending quite some time together, you'll know when you've hurt them, when you haven't, and when you are just trying to mentally talk yourself out of trouble (Scott & Goldman, 2020).

Don't Apologize for These Things in Your Relationship

For those who apologize too much and don't know it yet, consider the following things that you should never apologize for in a relationship— it might be eye-opening for some of us who feel we need to over-adapt or change who we are. This indicates that there is a balance issue and that one partner's individuality, or personality is being compromised.

1. Don't apologize for being quirky. Don't apologize for having natural, individual qualities that most people don't have, even if they are very, very unique, so to say. This should really go without saying. Your partner should've been aware of these quirks from the beginning of your relationship, except if you've developed a personality or character trait overnight. Apologizing for being quirky is the same as apologizing for being you, and that is simply unacceptable in an intimate and long-term relationship. Your partner should also not be accepting these apologies. If you are doing this, you need to spend some time developing a love and appreciation for yourself. Self-care can help you, and so should your partner

with unwavering support. The only exception, in this case, would possibly be if your quirks are a danger to others, malevolent in some nature, or illegal, and I cannot think of any good examples of any of those right now.

2. On a lighter note, many partners feel like they should apologize when they ask a question out of habit to the point that it becomes repetitive. This habit of apologizing is unhealthy because you are not really doing anything wrong. So, stop it! You are entitled to asking lots and lots of questions as the very basis of that action shows that you have an interest in your partner's opinion and preferences. The only scenario I'd approach separately is if you repeatedly ask questions because you don't listen to your partner's replies, in which case apologizing is still not the answer. Listening and remembering are.

3. You and your partner are different and have different interests, and these differences should be respected. Therefore, you should never feel like you should apologize for any type of interest or hobby you have or want to try. If it's a new one, it cannot possibly be so far removed from your personality that it's a total shock to your partner, can it? In any case, if it's not harming anyone, then there's no apology required. Sometimes, partners can hold each other back by making the other feel guilty for starting a new productive or healthy hobby, especially if they are feeling left behind. If this is the case and your partner is attempting to put you on a guilt trip because they are feeling left out, don't apologize because you feel sorry for them. Apologies are only used when required. Instead, try to include them or encourage them to also start a new hobby.

4. On we go to more touchy ones that many partners feel they need to apologize for and often do. Let's look at self-expression and expressing your opinion. Have you ever apologized for doing this? Maybe it will be easier to answer that

question after we've unobfuscated opinions from insults and critique. When it comes to these three forms of expression, the only time an apology would be warranted is if the comment was not made in good faith. If you had bad intentions by knowing that what you're going to say will hurt your partner, but you did it anyway in a very blunt and uncaring way, then I'd say it doesn't fall under this category. However, if you were expressing yourself honestly and earnestly and your partner happened to disagree with you, they should take it on the chin. You'll know when you are expressing an honest opinion and when you're making a targeted remark, and I'm sure no-one needs to tell anyone the second option is a no-no in relationships.

5. If you have a needy partner, it's difficult not to feel guilty when you need alone time. Especially when you see the disappointment on their face when you tell them you're just going to go do something—alone. This can be really difficult because you don't want to make your partner unhappy, but at the same time, you need that alone time really badly. What do you do? Anything but apologize. You can try talking to your partner; however, I'm sure that if you've been together for a while, they understand why you take alone time. It may still make them sad when you do, though. Because you're not doing anything wrong (in fact, what you are doing is healthy for the relationship), there's no need to apologize. Just show some good old love.

6. Sometimes we make mistakes that are trivial, and most of us apologize for these mistakes out of habit. Do we really need to? An example of a trivial mistake is accidentally burning the potatoes. Really? No need to say sorry. I think most of us know this but apologizing in these situations is so completely ingrained in us that we just do it anyway without reflecting on what an apology actually is and what it is supposed to do in a

relationship. Keep apologies for "special occasions," so to speak, and not for trivial or accidental mistakes that will literally make no difference in your relationship. You may just need some extra ketchup.

Do you need to get rid of some unhealthy habits? It really sounds counterintuitive but apologizing all the time is going to cause more harm than good in a relationship and is definitely not healthy. It means that somewhere, something is being compensated for, and identifying this issue and dealing with it can make both partners happier and healthier. A great tool you can use to curb your apologizing addiction is mindfulness. Try to identify the reasons why you apologize unnecessarily and make a point of being aware of them. This can help stop yourself in your tracks or even in mid-apology because you've trained yourself to identify these situations. Looking at the reasons behind unnecessary apologies can also be good for self-development. Understanding your behavior helps you to move forward and improve yourself, and self-improvement shows that you are being proactive in your relationship. Talk to your partner about your habits and get their feedback about it if you want to. Their reactions can also tell you a lot about the way they perceive apologies and whether you are on the same page when it comes to understanding the requirements for apologies (Howard, 2018).

Remember the 5 Love Languages? Here Are the 5 Languages of Apology

Did you know that Gary Chapman also wrote about the 5 apology languages? Have you ever thought about apologies this way? It makes sense in a way, because even after an apology, situations aren't always cleared up. So, similar to a love language, you most likely have a specific apology language. They are not directly related to the love language types, but they also show that partners can interpret something as important as an apology in unique ways and may need additional information to effectively interpret each other's peace offerings. Because we're already familiar with Gary Chapman, we can dive straight in and take a look at the 5 apology languages.

An apology language has to do with how an individual gives or receives an apology and their perception of it. The concept and its explanation are set down in a book that Gary Chapman co-wrote with Jennifer Thomas, called *The Five Languages of Apology*. Similar to the 5 love languages, one can also take a quiz to find out what your dominant language of apology is, and you may or may not be surprised that we've mentioned these languages before. However, Chapman makes you think differently about these components of an apology as he interprets them as to how your partner wants you to tell them you're sorry and how you tell your partner that you're sorry. The five different languages of apology are:

1. The expression of regret: *I am ashamed of the way I treated you.*
2. Accepting responsibility: *I should've known better/it was wrong to do that.*
3. Feeling genuinely sorry/repent: *I can't imagine how it made you feel. I will never do that to you again.*
4. Restitution: *This is what I want to do to make it up to you.*
5. A request to be forgiven: *Can you find it in your heart to forgive me?*

As you will know, these are all components of a sincere apology. However, what Chapman argues is that every individual has a primary preference of what is most important to them in an apology. For example, for one person it may be how you're going to make it up to them while another wants the reassurance that you genuinely regret what you've done. It's an interesting take on completely deconstructing a sincere apology and applying it to our wants and needs in a relationship.

The Importance of Knowing You and Your Partner's Language of Apology

Digging this deep into what an apology is can only be good if you use the information wisely. If you know how your partner wants to be approached and what is important to them in an apology, this can quicken the healing process and aid forgiveness, which will encourage open conversation in a relaxed atmosphere. However, it may seem exactly the opposite of sincere to approach an apology so strategically. Is it? Well, sincerity comes from the inside and one's behavior is based on these inner feelings. If you are sincere in your apology, make it more focused to reassure your partner does not make it disingenuous; however, if you use this strategy to get what you want through an insincere apology, that would be the ultimate apology fraud. The key purpose of knowing the apology language of your partner and them knowing yours is to be able to apologize in a manner where both parties feel heard and valued.

If you have a different apology language than your partner, which is highly likely, it may not be a problem at all, or you may have to compromise. For example, finding out that the most important part of an apology for your partner is hearing how you're going to make it up to them may sound a bit vapid if your primary preference is the angelic "acceptance of responsibility." Remember that this is another opportunity for you to understand your partner and that wanting to know, first and foremost, what form the restitution will manifest in may be a psychological need that developed during childhood or after an unsuccessful previous relationship. No language is superior to another, and they are meant to be used so you can get closer to your partner and understand them better as a whole person. A great idea is to incorporate their love language when you are using their language of apology for the ultimate display of devotion and love. If you are committed to understanding your partner and you find that the love languages work well for you, this can make making up so much more productive. Always seek mutual understanding and, when in doubt, communicate openly and honestly (Andrews, 2020).

The Dark Side of an Apology

There's a reason why an apology is both famous and infamous. Apologies are often used to manipulate others, and as much as we don't want to focus on the negative, it is sometimes a proactive thing to do. Being able to identify when an apology is being used to manipulate you and knowing that a partner may not be likely to do it, but they are capable of doing it, is important relationship information. Why would a partner use an apology to manipulate you? It might be a spontaneous decision driven by the desperation that they instantly regret afterward. It may be to save face, to cover a white lie, or to cover a bigger lie. In the end, an apology, which is meant to restore harmony and trust in a relationship, can be used for selfish purposes. If you are receiving an apology meant to manipulate, it can fall within one of these categories:

1. The first manipulative apology is one made out of selfishness. In other words, what your partner is really saying to you is that they don't want to feel guilty or be bothered with this issue anymore. Sometimes people do this because they genuinely can't seem to grasp what they did wrong, and they want to get rid of the unpleasantness by offering a hollow apology so things can go on as per normal. In this case, there is most likely a big communication problem in the relationship that needs to be ironed out as one or both partners don't appear to grasp each other's basic wants and needs and what they translate into. If your partner acts like this, try to find the reason why they are offering these hollow apologies before giving them a "bad person" stamp on the forehead. What they are doing is most definitely selfish and wrong, but their core intentions may not be to hurt you with a slapdash apology if there is just a deeper misunderstanding about wants and needs. In other words, this apology may come from a place of frustration as they don't know what else to do in such a situation. Either way, if you get

the feeling that your partner is just saying sorry to get the issue out of the way, there is a reason to investigate. Your first reaction may be anger at their insolence, but by lashing out, you won't get the answers you need. Take up the issue in a constructive conversation where both partners get a chance to express themselves openly and honestly.

2. The second type of manipulative apology is one that may indicate some reasonably serious issues. In this case, your partner may offer an apology, but what they are actually saying is "this conversation is over" or that they don't want to deal with this issue anymore. If your partner genuinely did something wrong and they cut you off with a fake apology, you need to have a serious conversation. Ways to identify this kind of apology is, for example, if you were to bring up the situation in the future or refer to it, it may upset your partner and even trigger them. This is because a healthy apology opens up that door to discussion and closure, which makes the topic open for discussion at a later stage, but if the issue was never resolved and only swept under the rug by an 'apology,' bringing it up again is going to make your partner nervous and angry.

3. The third and very sneaky manipulative apology is when an individual apologizes but gets you to be the actual apologizer in the end. This happens often, and I'm sure most of us have experienced it before. It goes something like this: "OK, I'm sorry that I said those things, but you know, you made me so angry that I couldn't help it." This person obviously wants you to apologize for making them angry. Did you make them angry on purpose? If not, then they are trying to manipulate you and place the blame on your shoulders. In this case, the apology is being forced on you because they can't or just don't want to take responsibility for what you've done. There is no other way but to sit this individual down and go through the whole debacle, discussing your role and their role, until the

conversation comes to a point where they cannot deny that they did something wrong.

4. The final manipulative apology is one that is used to control. If you think about it, all of the examples above are, in some way, a way to control the other party by offering a disingenuous apology. However, the apology can also be used to control another person by being used as a method of appeasement and nothing more. If you have or have had a controlling partner, this can or could have happened to you in the past. The only reason they apologize is so they can get you to do what they want. This method, like the previous one, is much darker, and if you've experienced this in your relationship or look back and see that it has happened before, you need to talk to your partner as a primary step (Desanctis, 2019).

Who could ever have thought a simple apology can be so complicated? As a child, your parents told you to say sorry, and you said sorry. That was enough. As adults in long-term relationships, we come to find that we've revolutionized the concept of the apology so it can be used for good and bad. Focus on the good and be aware of the bad. The most important word in this entire chapter remains 'sincerity.'

Chapter 7:

Who Wants a Baby?

Now, this can be a maker or breaker. However, most partners discuss their desire to have children before getting hitched. The question is whether they feel the same after a decade or two or even after only five years. Other circumstances that can change this romantic truce is the fact that one partner may experience infertility issues after marriage that could not be predicted. If this happens, what are your options? How will your partner feel about the fact that you don't prefer a natural birthing process? There are so many options and possibilities that having a baby can become an independent financial, ethical, and relationship goals discussion, each in their own respect. So, let's start with timing and how to handle the discussion about when to have a baby.

Is There a Perfect Time?

If only I had a nickel for every time someone carrying a screaming child or who is trying to walk with a toddler clinging to their foot told me that there's no perfect time to have a baby. I may not turn out to be stinking rich, but I could've counted them and told you how many times it's happened. You get individuals who meticulously plan the birth of their child according to several contributing factors, like whether they would be able to afford raising a child, if both partners are healthy enough to conceive and take up the challenge of parenthood, and some even assess the economic climate of the country they live in to decide if their child will have a future. On the other end of the baby-making spectrum, you get couples who take it easy, and then one day a baby pops out. Ta-da! And they appear to manage just as well as those meticulous planners, which is mostly barely. However, if you're looking for some sound advice and you do want to conduct some pre-baby planning, there are a few helpful main ideas that you can consider.

First, you may be at your physical best in your twenties, but what about your work situation? For most couples, being in their twenties means that they are starting out financially and they may not have the resources to have children at this age. This is a legitimate issue to consider, especially if you take the cost of living into account and how adding another family member would affect your financial freedom. If this is important to you, you need to discuss it as partners and prospective parents, but keep in mind that even the most meticulous financial planning cannot predict the future, if that's what you are looking at. So, don't rely on the thought of "Next year we'll be in a better position," and then when next year comes, you find yourself procrastinating again. Try to be decisive if you know it's what you want and actively work towards contributing financially by setting goals so you can ultimately reach the point where you feel ready.

The upside for women getting pregnant when they are younger is that their bodies handle the stress of the pregnancy dynamically and they bounce back much quicker after giving birth. If this is important for you as an individual who wants to have a child through pregnancy, you need to consider your age as one of the contributing factors. There are also more risks for the mother and baby in cases where the pregnancy occurs at an older age (Sinrich, 2018).

When it comes to adoption, the process is just as exciting and possibly as scary as giving birth. Are there things you need to know or consider before adopting? It depends on couple to couple, but here are some foundational ideas you can definitely look at if you want to adopt.

You and your partner need to explore your own emotional limits before adopting. It depends on the age of the child you want to adopt, but an adoption comes with different situations. For example, the child may come from an abusive home, they may have other siblings which may stay behind if you decide to adopt them, and these things can make you emotionally vulnerable and complicate the parenting process. If you are already in the initial stages of an adoption process and you have a specific child in mind, create a mental idea of how the child will fit into the family dynamics.

Adoption will raise a difficult question that may anger some and some may view this question dismissively. However, it remains important to do some introspection and to be honest with yourself about this because there's no shame in it. Consider exploring the idea of loving a child who is not yours as your own. Put yourself, as a parent, in the most difficult situation you can imagine and ask yourself if you will be able to love this child unconditionally. Parental, unconditional love may come later as you get to know your adoptive child, but you can show loyalty and dedication to them by making a decision of commitment at the start (Powell, 2016).

One thing you should prepare yourself for if you want to adopt is questions from other people (Powell, 2016). People are naturally curious, and they mostly don't have an ounce of tact when the curiosity bug bites. You can expect a spectrum of intrusive questions like, "Why doesn't your child look like you?" or "What's wrong? Why did you decide to adopt?" If you are a same-sex couple, you may even receive some rude questions like, "Do you think it's okay for a child to have two fathers?" Alternatively, you may just get that "look," but that look can say a lot. You can set an example for your child by just brushing off these birdbrained questions, and don't even humor them by giving them another thought. Just as you'll get fools who ask rude questions, you will encounter wonderfully supportive individuals who have a sense of openness and understanding. Luckily, some people do understand that not everyone's choices are everyone's business.

Finally, you and your partner need to decide how you are going to do this together. An unplanned pregnancy can just happen one day with a baby popping out nine months later, but with adoption, you have the opportunity to plan your collaboration strategy with your partner. You can collect literature and self-help books to read and hold discussion sessions. This can help you sort out any disagreements before you embark on your co-parenting mission. You can plan your discussions specifically around the age of the child you want to adopt and the challenges that this will pose for you as partners. Remember to make a truce that you will both stick to the decisions you make and not flip when confronted with a difficult situation.

Do We Both Want the Same Thing?

If you've decided that you want a baby and you've either made specific plans or you've decided to go with the flow, there are still some measures you can take to ensure that your relationship stands the test of time after the arrival of the little one. Even though becoming a parent may be one of the best things that happens to you, it may not be the best thing that's going to happen to your marriage if you don't try to mindfully balance out the two components. Being parents on the one side and being lovers on the other can require some juggling skills that you can either practice beforehand or learn to do while being thrown into the deep end. Having children has even been likened to relationship bootcamp, and even though other parents can give you advice on their experiences, your experience in your relationship may not be quite the same. To make sure that your relationship survives the new addition, let's look at some child-proofing ideas while there's still time.

You and your partner must take some selfish time and not feel guilty about it! When having a baby, it's difficult not to feel guilty when leaving your young one with your parents or a sitter even for a few hours, but just think about the small amount of time you are dedicating to your partner compared to before you had a baby. You guys need to talk about grownup stuff without being interrupted by a nappy emergency or projectile vomiting. A happy baby is raised by happy parents, and happy parents make time for themselves and their relationship. The best thing you can do for your child is to show them how much you care for each other and how much you love each other.

Next, when your baby comes, you need to prepare yourself for some serious compartmentalizing and structuring in your time. There are times when your baby has to be your first priority, but you need to use the time in between to do other important things like self-care, organizing the home if you're into that, and having partner-time. Your schedule may not be set and the same every day, so improvisation can go a long way. When you see those eyes becoming heavy with sleep, go and stuff the overloaded laundry basket into the washing machine and put on that matcha and cucumber mask you've been wanting to try out. Take turns during the night to get up if your baby needs to be fed or if there's a nappy change requirement. Most importantly, don't start an argument about you doing more than your partner. To childproof your relationship, you should consider making a truce beforehand about sharing the coming responsibilities, and these promises need to be kept showing your devotion, commitment, and love toward one another.

Another strategy that can really help new parents in the first years of parenthood is having a backup. You know, someone who they can call when they need help. If you can recruit multiple backups, then that's even better. Are there family members who live close by? Do you have a nephew or niece that's old enough to babysit and who would like to be handsomely rewarded? By knowing that these individuals are close and maybe just a phone call away can provide you with the freedom to be more spontaneous if you want to spend some time alone, and they can also be a source of emotional support. Studies indicate that, without an external support system, parents tend to experience depression, which may be due to a feeling of helplessness.

The next one may be really hard, but it's important for preventing your baby completely taking over your relationship with your partner. It's really important to keep your bed reserved for you and your partner only. This is the one room that is yours and yours only, so keep this space sacred and private. With this suggestion, I mean that it's best if the baby has its own room with a baby monitor that will still make you feel connected and so you'll still know if it needs you. Co-sleeping may not seem harmful at first, but it can cause you and your partner to drift apart; mainly for the same reason we discussed earlier, which is not spending enough alone time together. Co-sleeping is one of those things that can happen suddenly and spontaneously, especially when your child becomes a toddler, and while one partner may be ok with it, the other may have issues but are hesitant to voice their opinion. You may, for example, think it's just going to be this one night and then you'll make sure they sleep in their own bed again, but will it be that easy for you? A parent's first instinct is to protect, and how better than to hold your baby in your arms? This can be really hard, so it's important to discuss this with your partner beforehand as part of how you're going to keep things consistent after the new addition arrives for the sake of your relationship.

Remember to show your partner that you're still on board by expressing your appreciation and gratitude for their efforts. Whether it's offering to look after the baby so you can get a session in at the gym or cleaning a particularly stinky diaper, this shows that both of you still want the same thing (Fetters, 2014).

Where Do Babies Come From?

Apart from the occasional stork delivering new little ones at our front doors, there are many ways to "have a child," hence me putting the phrase in quotation marks. It doesn't matter what your gender identity or sexual preferences are; there is an option to bring a bundle of joy into your life. If you've discussed having a baby with your partner, you can look further into this section at all the options you have—that is, if using a stork doesn't fall within your frame of reference.

If you decide to choose a method that is non-traditional, in other words, not a pregnancy that results from sexual intercourse between a heterosexual couple with the aim to raise the child as their own, there are a few possible obstacles you can take note of and keep in mind. First, like heterosexual or CIS couples, non-heterosexual couples or LGBTQ couples can also experience issues like infertility, situational infertility, or one or both partners can be sterile, which can limit their options a bit more than it would with other couples. You may also have to deal with extra financial issues and legal procedures, depending on your choices.

One of the options available for couples who cannot conceive on their own is third party reproduction. As the name suggests, third-party reproduction requires a third person to provide either the sperm or egg, or to be a willing gestational carrier for you and your partner. Some couples choose to go with a known gestational carrier or donor, which means the third party is a person familiar or known to them. If you want the third party to be someone you know, you and your partner need to think carefully about the consequences of this decision and how it will affect your relationship with the third party. A known gestational carrier can bring some peace of mind, but the process can put a lot of strain on the relationship. This may even lead to subsequent legal issues if the known carrier or donor wants to change the terms of involvement they have in the future child's relationship or even claiming parental rights.

This may be why choosing an anonymous donor is generally a more traditional choice that carries less legal risks and possible conflict, which can ruin the whole process for the couple. In this case, the recipient/couple has no information about the donor and their identity. The closest you may come to knowing who your donor is is by possibly looking at a childhood or baby picture; otherwise, the couple and recipient will have not had any contact with the donor. This method is regarded to be the most risk-free option for parents who want to use third-party reproduction because it limits or completely rules out emotional and legal complications that could have arisen if the donor knew the recipient. However, if the donor is anonymous, this may not rule out all complications. After you've had the baby, your child may or may not wonder about their biological parent, depending on whether you decide to be open with them about this. You, as a couple, may always wonder about the donor of your child, and likewise, the donor may also always wonder about their child. This led to the development of more open third-party agreements, like using a semi-open donor or gestational carrier.

If you choose a semi-open arrangement, you'll have access to more information about the donor and also limited contact through making a semi-open arrangement. In a case like this, you will likely be working through a law firm or another type of intermediary like a donor agency. In a semi-open agreement, the donor will be eligible to receive information like whether their donation led to a pregnancy and birth, and they can also receive a photo of the baby from the intended parents, depending on what is stipulated in the contract. Personal details like phone numbers and physical addresses, however, are never shared in a semi-open arrangement. A semi-open arrangement can also include stipulations that allow the child to reach out to the donor, and this is usually linked to when the child reaches a specific age.

Finally, you, as prospective parents, can choose a fully open arrangement with your gestational carrier or donor. This means that the donor you choose is not someone you've known for a long time like with a known donor or carrier, but this agreement allows the two parties to meet and interact. The nature of the relationship between the donor/carrier and prospective parents are also ongoing due to the nature of their open contract. It is, for example, not uncommon for the donor and intended parents to go to doctor's appointments together, and future contact between the donor and intended parents/family may also be stipulated in the contract. What this means is that a relationship is allowed to develop, to some level, between the donor/carrier and the intended parents and child.

Let's move on by looking at In-Vitro Fertilization (IVF). This method includes harvesting eggs from a woman's ovaries and conducting the unification process with the sperm in a lab setting. An embryo is then planted back into the woman's uterus so she can experience a relatively normal pregnancy. The IVF process links to using a donor or gestational carrier as we discussed earlier, but it is a multifaceted process on its own that provides different options for different couples. IVF also allows for the cryopreservation of extra embryos.

One IVF option to consider is Reciprocal IVF. This process is perfect for a lesbian couple who both want to play a role in the creation of their child. During Reciprocal IVF, eggs would be harvested from one partner for stimulation, and the embryo would be transferred to the uterus of the other partner so a pregnancy can take place. This means that Reciprocal IVF allows one mother to be genetically related to the baby, while the other has the privilege to give birth. There are still choices involved that can be complicated or difficult for partners. For example, whose genes should the baby carry? The answer to this question can be personal or it may have a medical origin. A sperm donor is generally required for reciprocal IVF, so this decision can be based whether the couple wants an anonymous donor, a semi-open, or an open arrangement.

IVF can also be successful with an embryo donor. In this case, the embryo will be implanted in a gestational carrier or in the womb of one of the partners. However, if you choose IVF with an embryo donor, you need to be aware of the fact that the child will not be genetically related to you or your partner. This is because neither the egg nor the sperm came from you or your partner. This, however, is just a need-to-know and has nothing to do with the fact that you can still raise the child as your own and love it as your own. Because embryo donors tend to be couples who are, themselves, struggling to conceive, the chances of a successful pregnancy using an embryo donor may be slightly lower than when using an egg donor. It ultimately depends on the donor. In the case of a same-sex lesbian couple, the embryo will be implanted into the uterus of the partner who wants to go through the pregnancy. Alternatively, if it's a same-sex gay couple, a gestational carrier will be required fulfill the pregnancy. An embryo donor is not everyone's first choice but is available to couples who experience fertility or other medical issues, and it enables them to still experience parenthood.

If you're part of a heterosexual couple who also want to use IVF but need an egg donor, you can still use the sperm of the intended father, so the child is genetically related to one of the parents. In the case of a homosexual lesbian couple, they may require both a sperm and egg donor if both partners cannot provide an egg, or alternatively go for an embryo donor.

Another option you can look at is adoption or foster care. It is a myth that homosexual and LGBTQ couples cannot adopt as any couple or have the right to apply for adoption. When it comes to the different ways you can choose to go about it, there are plenty. Some pathways are more expensive than others, and some differ in type. For example, you can approach a private agency, through a private individual on a person-to-person basis or self-matching adoption, through the state, or you can choose the foster care system. Some adoption avenues may be less discriminating than others for LGBTQ individuals, like self-matching adoption. Some psychological issues may also arise when choosing to adopt older children. For example, the child may feel that the female counterpart of the adoptive parents, if the couple is a heterosexual couple, may be trying to take their mother's place. In such a case, it has been observed that a child adapts quicker when adopted by a single male. Whereas, if you aim to adopt a child who has been in several foster homes, they may need extra care and time to adjust to a more permanent setting (Gurevich, 2020).

No matter how you choose to have your child, the aim is to expand your family and bring happiness and fulfilment for you and your partner. A good start is to discuss all the available options and to do research so that you find the best agency or clinic that will cater to your individual needs.

Post-Baby Getaways and Dates

We can't end this chapter without discussing some naughty post-baby getaways. You won't be running down the street naked and wasted, but you'll be having some fun, nonetheless. You know, experiences where you can invent new inside jokes and precious memories, and even become the individuals you were when you first met. Here's to having a "I'm a new parent, so I'm being slightly responsible" date night!

After all those nights cooking or ordering in at home, and not really feeling like dining out, why don't you think out of the box and go for a cooking class? You can spend lots of time arguing about the type of food you want to learn cooking and then have a ball playing with your hands and getting down and dirty. Attending a couples' cooking class and learning something new like making pasta is always a fun way to bond as a couple. You get to eat the cheesy reward afterwards—if it's a success, that is. Chances are you'll arrive back home with a full belly and proud of your team effort.

Alternatively, you can try some outdoor activities. The activity you choose should preferably depend on your fitness level. A good example is going for a bike ride, taking a hike, or taking a bottle of bubbly with you that you can sip while watching the scenic sunset. Try your local tourist website for some neat ideas. Take this time to focus on each other while you're enjoying nature and try not to get too tipsy if you're going to be cycling back (Koenig, 2019).

One idea I especially like is spontaneously planning a trip to the most obscure place you can think of. That is, apart from your parents' bedroom. They'll most likely be looking after the baby for you (fingers crossed), so let's look elsewhere, shall we? Make a game out of it by having each of you write down the names of five obscure places, each on your own piece of paper, and then throw them all in a hat, beanie, plastic container, or whatever you can find that works. You can even use the diaper bag. Try not to choose a location that's on the other side of the world or one that may pose logistical obstacles. Now, you have to decide who's going to draw the winning ticket. I'll let you figure that one out. After you've established your trip to obscurity, take the next weekend off, hop on the plane or in the car, and go make memories like only you can.

Here's another idea; book a hotel room for the day! Take your partner and go spend a day in a luxury hotel. Make it your own secret mission and don't tell anyone about your plans. If the babysitter asks where you're going, tell her you've never seen an elephant, so you're going to the zoo. When you arrive in your room, do everything you've always wanted to do like jumping on the bed, harassing room service, watching R-rated movies together, and raiding the minibar. When you arrive, establish ground rules like immediately getting rid of your clothes and wearing only the robes provided or less. You can also make some other ground rules to make your stay more adventurous. Remember to wear sunglasses when checking in and out so you can look extra suspicious.

All of my suggestions seem to involve alcohol for some reason, but this one is also a great idea for an unforgettable outing. Consider visiting a winery or a distillery that's in your area for some fun tasting and pairing. How about going for something you've never tried before or visiting a new craft beer distillery? These venues usually have some fun pairing activities and restaurants you can visit after trying your cognac, wine, beer, vodka, tequila, MCC, or gin. Try every possible pairing and make sure to take a taxi. Two rules, though: stay with one drink and have a proper meal.

Chapter 8:

The Importance of Self-Care

While successful communication is an integral part of a healthy relationship, each partner has a responsibility not only to look after each other but also to look after themselves. Practicing self-care shows your partner that you have a sense of self-respect, you are willing to get up every morning and do what is necessary to keep the relationship alive, and that you love them enough to love yourself. Self-care goes more than skin deep and actually starts with your mindset. A healthy mind radiates through strength, patience, and care—towards yourself and others. If you think that you need some help with self-care, whether it is on a mental or physical level, here are some ideas and guidelines that you can use as inspiration to improve the way you feel about yourself and the way you feel about your relationship. Practicing self-care also means that you are setting a good example for those around you, like your family and friends. This is because you exude positivity and confidence if you look after yourself and you are positive about yourself. In order to practice mental and physical self-care successfully when you are in a relationship or have a family, it's important to set practical boundaries for those around you that provide you with the space to practice self-care. When you think about prioritizing time with your partner and also having a baby around when that happens, then squeezing in self-care can be difficult, and it is often neglected because you want to put your partner and child first. Don't do it! If you want to support those around you in times of need, you need to be healthy and actively working towards maintaining a healthy mind and body. If you think that others' needs are more important than yours most to all of the time, then your relationship may move into an unhealthy space.

Mental Self-Care

Psychologists are confident about the fact that a lack of self-care can put a relationship under a lot of strain. The first thing one tends to think, especially when it comes to mental self-care is that it's selfish and self-centered to harbor such a mindset, especially if others are dependent on you. This is when the opposite is, in fact, true. People that actively practice self-care have the ability to be more productive, and they have more energy to tackle difficult situations, which are crucial skills in a relationship. If you love yourself, you have the capacity to love others more because there's no room for self-loathing or being overly critical. There are several things you can do to implement a continuous mental self-care routine that start with the smallest of phrases to taking some time off doing something that you enjoy. Don't neglect any hobbies you had prior to your marriage or when you became a parent. When was the last time you picked up a book and just took half an hour to an hour reading something that you enjoy? Do you still get your favorite magazine every month or week, or did that habit mysteriously disappear? Another way to practice self-care is to experience the feeling of victory after learning something new. Have you ever been fascinated in something, but you never thought it's really worth the time to learn about it? I've always been fascinated in ancient history and archeology, and I love following related accounts on social media. So, I always find a link on one of the pages that leads me to a fascinating story about how people used to live thousands of years ago. Finding something that makes you think further and look at the world in awe helps to create a sense of perspective about your life and how you can live it to the fullest. An even better idea is to take a self-day and visit a gallery or a museum where you can look at thought-provoking visuals that will nourish your soul and leave you awe-inspired.

Another underrated activity that is great for mental self-care is to keep a journal. This practice seems to go in and out of fashion, but if you make time for it and do it conscientiously, it can be a great way to rid yourself of frustrations and express yourself on a completely non-judgmental blank page (Roberts, 2015). That is, if you want to do it the traditional way by writing by hand. You can also keep a journal on your PC, tablet, and phone, and there are many journal apps available with intelligent features that make journaling interesting and fun. I still, however, choose the old-fashioned pen-to-paper method. One's handwriting is in itself a form of self-expression, and I like to doodle at the top-right part of the page while I formulate my sentences. Other ways of letting out expressive energy is by painting or drawing. If you feel like this is not for you because you don't see yourself as "artistic," keep in mind that the purpose of the activity is to express yourself and not to create a society-approved masterpiece. For some inspiration on expressionist and abstract art, you can look at the works of Egon Schiele, Jackson Pollock, Frida Kahlo, Willem de Kooning, and Malcolm Liepke. These artists all have different techniques and styles, but they are all expressive artists. Some of the art may be ugly, some may be confusing, and some may seem pointless. But, that's how you realize that you can create your own art without judgment; your art is a true reflection of you and doesn't need to meet society's standards or require their understanding.

A self-care must-have that we also need to add is taking a nap. There's no underestimating taking a nap. Just make sure that it's a mindful nap and that you're not using the time to worry about stuff. If you're going to take a nap, get your mind prepared for your mental relaxation shutdown session. After lying down, let your thoughts and worries float away on a little cloud. You can even say "bye-bye" or "later, gator!" Allow yourself to feel free from worries as you float away for a short powernap. By letting go of your worries before you go to sleep through the emptying of your mind, your sleep will be more restful, and you will wake up invigorated and ready to take on the havoc that's been wrought during your nap. A trick you can try is to set a different alarm sound than the one that wakes you up in the morning for when you're finished with your nap. This can help you wake up in a better mood, especially if you're not a morning person. Try the tinkling of a little bell or a soft melody that will ease you out of your sleep.

Alternatively, look for audio recordings that support sleep and also a natural waking up process.

If you're not into power-napping but you want to take some time to relax your mind, you can also try meditation. Some people always wake up feeling groggy, so if that's you, maybe you can consider switching off your mind while staying awake. Meditation involves finding a space where you can experience a sense of calm and where there are no distractions. Meditation is very effective if you can try to find a space for yourself first thing in the morning. The effects of meditating before you begin your day adds a preparatory calmness which you can use to tackle obstacles you may experience during your day like conflict or other issues with mindfulness and an open heart. If you like the idea of meditation and making a habit of it, you can boost its effectiveness by practicing in the same space and at the same time, whichever time and level of frequency you choose to do it. Even if it's not in the morning as suggested, keeping to a specific time will create a scheduled and private time you can look forward to. Don't feel you have to sit in a yogi position to mediate. The most important part of mediation is that your body is relaxed and comfortable and that nothing is distracting you from the experience. However, if you like sitting cross-legged, go right ahead and be as comfortable as you can. Now, while you are meditating, focus on easy, consistent, and deep breathing. Breathing calmly brings down your heart rate, promotes relaxation, and helps you to focus on the natural way your body functions. If you are a newbie at mediation, you may struggle with "getting into it" at first, and it's possible that you may become frustrated with yourself and even become anxious because you don't seem to get the results you expected. This is completely normal, and by keeping in mind why you are taking this time for yourself and allowing yourself to gently slip into the act of positive focus will give you a feeling of accomplishment every time you go back to practice. Finally, after you feel that you are ready to move on, keep the peaceful feeling with you and apply that clarity of mind on every task that lies before you ("The Top 13 Meditation Tips," 2020).

A final mental exercise that should never be overlooked is actively appreciating the things that you do for yourself and for others. You have the right to pat yourself on the back if you've achieved a milestone in your life, whether personal or career-wise. Actively working on your self-esteem is important because, even though those around you love and appreciate you, they may not always be so tuned into your wants and needs. We all have our own goals and plans on how to achieve them, and even though you and your partner have shared goals, you'll also have some of your own. Allowing yourself positivity and self-appreciation will help you achieve those goals, and the subsequent sense of achievement and self-appreciation will shine through. If you've finally figured out how to deal with your boss's nasty and rude assistant at work and she is now treating you with respect, pat yourself on the back—you've mastered a valuable communication skill. If you've been trying to make a good soufflé for ages and it finally came out all cushy and delicious, congratulate yourself on your budding culinary skills. Finally, if you've decided to take those running shoes out of the closet and you just completed running five miles for the first time, don't immediately go and eat a huge burger because you might throw up. Do congratulate yourself and know that you are showing your body love and care by doing this.

Physical Self-Care

Mental self-care should go hand-in-hand with physical self-care, and the two can work in on one another and complement each other. For example, you can go for a manicure or a pedicure to make yourself beautiful and leave the salon feeling better about yourself, thus also boosting your self-esteem. Physical self-care is a way to show that your mental state is positive and healthy, but that doesn't mean that you should completely abandon the practice of mental self-care altogether. Let's look at ways you can activate your complementary process to ultimately be the best partner you can be.

The best and most basic form of self-care is to take that long bath or shower, use your favorite products, and cover yourself with nice-smelling creams and lotions. I'm not only referring to women here. Every person has a different routine, but just doing it regularly forms a solid basis for physical self-care (Roberts, 2015). Something you can add to your bath or shower routine is a short stretch. You can do your stretching routine before or after but doing it before and feeling those muscles relax and unwind in the hot water is just the incarnation of bliss. If you want to compile your own stretching routine, looking at yoga asanas is always a great idea. They mobilize the spine and hips, and there are poses that don't require you to fold yourself into a pretzel. Try a downward-facing dog, a half-pigeon, a happy baby, child's pose, and a ragdoll or forward fold.

Physical activity is also a winner (Roberts, 2015). For self-care, exercise doesn't need to be an hour-long session at the gym six times a week. However, for exercise to be effective, you need to feel a sense of accomplishment or refreshment afterwards. Just get that heart rate up by taking a brief walk, a bike ride, conducting a spring clean, or doing some gardening. How about a dance class? One of those you do in front of the TV while your partner needs to go sit in another room for you to shake it. There are so many options that this one is really up to you. You can go walk the dogs, do jumping lunges down the hall—this is your call. As long as you feel those endorphins working afterwards!

After you've done your highly individualized physical exercise routine, you can further practice some physical self-care by doing something with your friends (Roberts, 2015). Plan something fun like a themed dinner party or a night out where you can let go and enjoy the diversity of your friends' personalities. Put on some nice-looking attire, do your hair, put on your favorite aftershave or perfume, and have a night to remember. Enjoy looking your best and the preparatory process you underwent to carefully and meticulously become this glammed-up version of yourself. Feeling and looking fabulous is the point here because you don't get to do this every day. Take pictures to remember your experience and how gorgeous you looked.

Finally, just like you take your bath or shower regularly, focus on maintaining a consistent grooming habit. Go for regular haircuts, style your hair the way you like it, trim that beard and use your favorite ultra-nourishing beard oil, and do the wax and tint when things start to look a bit fluffy. Use products that smell nice and that nourish your skin. Finally, don't skip a session. Even if you're feeling down. You're going to feel so much better and love yourself so much more.

Couples' Self Care

Another approach you can add to your self-care routine is to not only limit it to having alone time. However, having some alone time is highly recommended and should not be compromised for other activities unless they are very high on your priority list. You can also practice self-care as a couple. Couples' self-care brings a new dimension of self-care into your relationship and can bring you and your partner closer together; however, you need to be in a space in your relationship where both of you feel comfortable with couples' self-care. For example, if you practice individual self-care on a regular basis, then couple's self-care can be a natural next step for you because you've purposefully taken the time to nourish yourself from the inside, and this means that you are ready to bond and nourish your relationship. However, if you're not that active when it comes to personal self-care, you may want to focus on that first so that you can find yourself, your inner balance, and feel confident and whole as a human being. On the other hand, as you already know, everyone is different, so starting with couple's self-care may just help you get back into your solo self-care routine faster. The idea of couples' self-care may seem counterintuitive when looking at some of the reasons why one would do self-care activities alone. However, they can add a special dimension and depth to your relationship that only the two of you will understand.

The difference between couples' self-care and going on a date is that couples' self-care is specifically aimed at self-improvement, relationship improvement through a deeper connection, and doing fulfilling activities that are not necessarily materialistic or recreational in nature. Couples' self-care can simply be rituals that you practice every day and don't need to be a carefully planned, super-luxurious date night. To bring perspective to this effective relationship-building or maintenance tool, let's look at a few ways in which you can practice couples' self-care.

Let's first look at some fun self-care activities that you and your partner can do together to strengthen your bond. You may be surprised at what some of these activities are. For example, a great couples' self-care session is to take the entire Saturday and binge-watch a series you both love but don't have time to watch during the week. I know, self-care is supposed to resemble mainstream healthy habits, right? Wrong. Be a couch potato with your partner and enjoy doing absolutely nothing except analyzing all the characters as well as the plot of the show you've both been wanting to watch for so long. Make yourself snacks; they can be very healthy or you can have some junk food, as long as there's not a trace of negativity, guilt, stress, worry, or any other feelings that will cause your couples venture to backfire. This type of activity is necessary, especially if both of you are overworked and feel a bit disconnected. Not only will chilling on the couch in your PJ's bring down your stress levels but you will also get to reconnect and have some essential and intimate experiences that will make you remember all the reasons why you decided to hook up with your partner for the long haul.

Let's look at some healthy ideas like yoga. Have you ever tried yoga alone? How about with your partner? Couples' yoga is something that is both intimate on several levels and also great for you physically. Almost like sex. If you've never done yoga before, consider attending a yoga class together, but don't try couples' yoga right away. You need to oil those joints and strengthen those tendons first! Doing yoga with your partner can be fun in so many ways while also being mentally and physically therapeutic. If you're the competitive type, then go to see how much you can gain from the class physically and mentally to improve your relationship instead of comparing posture and poses. Focus on yourself but know that your partner is right there next to you doing the same thing in the name of your relationship. Make a mental connection as you strive to become stronger and better as individuals and as a unit. After savasana, you'll feel like a new person, and make sure to share that outpouring of positive energy with your partner as you encourage them to do the same.

Now that we're on the topic of exercise, a great couples' self-care activity is to take part in a mini marathon, a color run, or even a themed race. The best part about it is that you're in it together, so if there's a swarm of super-muscular, tanned Adonises swanning past you, you can share your pre-rehearsed inner smirk and just go at your own pace. Have a conversation, have a laugh, or go for the people-watching if you're not into athletic activities. If you are, go for the race—it's as simple as that. If the focus remains on your relationship, it's a win-win, and by showing each other you can achieve anything you set your minds to, you'll reach a sense of accomplishment that will bolster your relationship strength to dizzying heights. Sometimes, you need to show each other you can conquer common relationship issues by accomplishing wacky endeavors like mini marathons. They give back the trust and the sense of camaraderie you need to tackle other relationship issues (Holl, 2018).

Let's move on to less exerting efforts and look at smaller, more frequent activities you can focus on as a couple to instill self-care. You and your partner can make time for each other in mutually agreed times to discuss important aspects of your relationship. These practices will keep you focused on the future and common goals you have and ensure that you communicate about them regularly so your mind can be at ease that the consensus is still there. So, you and your partner can show care and devotion toward each other and your relationship by frequently discussing your relationship goals and journey. You can also review your goals and set new ones if your current goals feel outdated, especially if there has been a significant change in your lives that affects your goals. An example of such a change can be a new job, relocating, or deciding to have a baby. The point is that setting aside that time and devoting it to discuss your relationship with your partner develops true couples' self-care in your relationship that will make your bond stronger in the long run.

Another rewarding couples' self-care activity is identifying a project you both like and starting and completing it. This can be anything, from working through a recipe book or blog to doing some DIY things around the house. Alternatively, if you have space, you can start your own garden or do a hanging garden against your wall. Whatever brings both of you joy, instills a sense of teamwork, and showcases some of your skills, make use of it and it will be a great way to initiate a bonding process that ends with a sense of accomplishment. Trying some new recipes is my personal favorite, especially if I can add dessert to the menu. Go wild and have fun. You're with your best friend. Cherish every moment.

The next option is not for everyone, but there are definitely some couples that are into reading motivational books for advice on self-improvement. If you fit this description, why not do it together and discuss your experiences from the book? You can do this chapter-by-chapter or you can decide to finish the whole book first and then give each other insight. Not only will you learn something from the book, but you will also learn from each other's interpretations and from your own. It's a great way to deepen your understanding of your partner while doing something meaningful together that is aimed at self-improvement and the improvement of your relationship.

A fun one but one that you may not do on a regular basis is making a 'thing' out of planning a getaway or your next vacation. By 'thing' I mean thorough research, looking at reviews, price comparison versus amenities offered, different locations you've always dreamed of visiting—you get the idea. Create a whole doc or sheet on your laptop or iPad and go wild. Start quite some time before you go, especially if you're looking at places that are very popular and are likely to be fully booked. Listen to each other's wants and needs, try to get a bang for your buck and your budget, and see the beauty in the situation you are in. You may not be extremely wealthy, or there may be other shortcomings that you will notice during your vacation planning, but accepting them and appreciating them just as much as all the wonderful things you love about your relationship is the reason you're doing this together. Compromise, teamwork, and quality time spent together planning quality time that you're going to be spending together. If you love Googling everything, you're going to love this self-care activity. You're not going to do this every day, so make it a ritual for the time you're doing it. Meet each other at a café for a beer or a coffee and spend some time doing top-secret, super-serious vacay planning (Magee, 2019).

Keep Your Sense of Style—It Rocks!

Who would've thought that you can use your sense of style to boost your self-care? A person's style is actually such an integral part of their individuality that losing it or having to get rid of it due to the demand of another can lead to a negative sense of self and even confusion. Here's how keeping and preserving your sense of style is good for you and for your relationship.

Being mindful and deliberate about what you wear, as your fashion sense is an important way of practicing self-care. It's not only about looking your best, but about being you and allowing yourself to be you. It's easy to fall into the habit of just throwing on something in the morning just because you can't go to work naked and hoping that someone will think your outfit works. But, where's the care in that? Are you upholding and maintaining your sense of style by doing this? We just mentioned dressing up in something special for a night out with friends as a form of self-care. However, during those days when you have to go through the mundanities of life, do you bother making an effort with your sense of style? Dressing according to your personal style is like creating a painting that expresses your personality and mood. Being expressive is a form of self-care. Being able to showcase your uniqueness makes you value your sense of creativity and justify all the time you spend looking at fashion blogs, vlogs, and online shopping sites. Dressing deliberately doesn't only make you feel good, but it shows your partner that you care about yourself and that you care about being the best other half you can be.

You can make self-care and style fun and adventurous by trying out new ideas and styles. If they work for you, incorporate them into your wardrobe. If they don't, that's okay too. It's all about realizing that you can decide who you are, what you want to express through your style, and how you want to do it. A concept known as enclothed cognition plays an important role in style and self-care. This concept represents two independent factors related to style impacting each other, which are the physical experience of wearing clothes and the symbolic meaning that clothes can have ("Fashion as a Self-Care Tool," 2020). Although these factors may seem far removed, they both have an effect on how our sense of style can act as a form of self-care. To have the ultimate self-care experience, clothes should both be comfortable and be a reflection of one's personality.

When was the last time that you got yourself something that is a true reflection of who you are? Is your wardrobe currently full of baby-proof t-shirts and wide-legged chinos? Unless that's who you truly are, take a leap of faith and get yourself something that reflects your soul. Start small by accessorizing. Get earrings that reflect your beautiful eyes. Get yourself a new pair of boots or sneakers. Start now and get your sense of style back on track. People will notice. Your partner will notice. You'll love yourself and be loved for expressing how authentic you are.

Share Your Care

After you've felt love for yourself again, appreciated what you do for yourself and others again, and experienced the beauty of being you, you can experience the ultimate form of self-love by sharing your positivity and love with others. One of the most fulfilling acts of self-care is doing something for someone else (Roberts, 2015). An act of kindness is a reflection of an individual's level of self-care and their desire to share their positivity with others. It can be big, or it can be small. Help an older person to carry their bags to their car. Pick up something that the person in front of you dropped. Buy some food for the homeless man on the street corner. Or you can choose to spend a day helping at the local animal shelter. Watching your health heal and empower others is the most powerful form of self-care there is. However, you need to have it inside you already before you can genuinely spread it to others. You can even do this aspect of self-care development with your partner to give back to others as a couple.

Chapter 9:

Quirky Date Ideas

In this chapter, we are not going to discuss anything that comes close to a normal date. We're going to turn the "generic date night" upside down. When you go on a normal date, there are things you rely on, like the normalcy of the situation, that keeps you and your partner in your comfort zones. For example, it's normal to go to dinner and the movies, and you and your partner know how to act and behave in such a situation. But what if you wanted to leave that comfort zone and test new and absurd waters just to see how you and your partner can handle and improvise these situations? It's not really a difficult test, it's just a matter of adapting to a new situation, understanding it, and using it for relationship-building and having fun. That's why we're calling them "quirky date ideas."

"Quirky" is the closest we're going to come to describing these date ideas. If you try out some of these ideas, you genuinely have a wacky spontaneous side and a willingness to try something new! What's your idea of a perfect date? Dinner? Going to a big baseball game or a music festival? Let's flip that around. Then around again. Your quest for quirky date night is to choose an activity you can do as a couple that is completely outside of the normal dating stratosphere. This means that it's up to you to transform and renew this experience, which will not be anything close to a generic perfect date, and you need to make it work as a couple by improvising, and subsequently you will have loads of fun. I dare you to go on one of these quirky dates. You may even want to try a second and a third one after you've realized that the fun part of a date is not necessarily the expensive food or swanky décor, but how much fun you can have with your partner while doing something absolutely ridiculous. Pick a date and time, once a week or month, and prepare to be quirked-out.

The first quirky date option of many to come is to take some chalk and become performing artists on your local sidewalk ("200 Date Ideas - The Only List You'll Need to Find the Perfect Date Idea," n.d.). Not the one next to your house, of course. Go all-out Picasso on your local residents and draw some amazing and memorable art. You can even draw a few circles and triangles and play hopscotch. Alternatively, you can be a poet of note and write some gibberish poetry. Make sure that it's legible for all the curious passers-by to see.

The second quirky date option is to make a list of ten YouTube how-to videos and randomly select one. The selection method is up to you, of course, as long as it's quirky. This means that you are going to make whatever the person on the video you chose is making ("200 Date Ideas - The Only List You'll Need to Find the Perfect Date Idea," n.d.). Keep in mind that, when you choose the ten options initially, you need to choose videos that are contextually viable. You don't want to end up trying to build a steam engine or follow along on a tutorial about how to iron your clothes properly. Make it fun. A good idea is to look for recipe videos or other useful tutorials that are simple but fun to make. Have a blast testing out your teamwork skills and comparing your end result to the one in the video. Finally, don't forget to give your end product a rating out of 10.

Your third quirky date mission is to make a list of ridiculous tasks and see how many of them you can complete in a certain amount of time. If you want to make it a fun and relaxed outing with a few spurts of desperation, I'd say it would make a great Saturday morning or evening outing, depending on your tasks. Think along the lines of driving around until you've spotted three cars that are the same model and color. Then, you can move on to the next task, which could be buying hotdogs at a specific hotdog stand. When you've completed mission number two, you can move on to mission number three, which can be locating an unknown object in an unknown location. This may take a while, though, so it's entirely up to you. Be as random as possible and have as much fun compiling your mission list as you will while completing each task. You can even consider adding time limits for tasks where you need to locate or look for random objects to make it even more interesting. Take your mission very seriously while simultaneously having tons of fun and be sure to tick off all completed tasks on a list you can keep as a souvenir.

Let's add a creepy and macabre quirky date option for those with a darker sense of adventure. Pick a day and time, put on your black attire, and visit a cemetery near you. Take a picnic basket if you like, preferably with some wine, which you'll need. Your mission is to choose specific graves and figure out each person's life story and how they died. Make sure to stare the gravestone straight in the face to obtain as much information as possible. What is the story of Lily Jones' life? Was she the adulterous scarlet woman who tried to break up the marriage of poor Mr. and Mrs. Pembridge's from the far corner of the cemetery? Who else fell prey to her charms? I knew it! Mr. Schmidt's trying to hide behind that tree! Don't move Mr. Schmidt, we're coming for you! No disrespect towards those who have passed, of course. Before you know it, you'll be playing gravestone Cluedo in no time and having a blast. This one will require a lot of imagination and an open mind, though. If this option is too macabre for you, you can move on to the next one.

The fifth quirky date option actually includes going on a normal date, but you're not going to look normal. Book a table at your favorite restaurant and go for dinner wearing clothes that you would never, ever, otherwise wear in your life. If going to a familiar restaurant is too daunting, try one on the other side of town where nobody will recognize you. The fun part is the dressing up part. You can decide to go in costumes, you can each create a ridiculous outfit for the other to wear, or you can visit a thrift shop and buy the most mismatched, confusing ensembles you can think of. The trick here, like with all the quirky dates, is that you have to emerge yourself into the theme completely alongside your partner; this is your adventure and you're going to do this as a team. You can use those sunglasses again if you feel you need to. Walk into the restaurant like you own it, act like you look fabulous while everyone else is looking ridiculous and have an extended five-course meal with a refill of your favorite drink always on its way.

Quirky date number six requires of you and your partner not to be any kind of history or art experts. That's because you are going to visit a gallery and pretend to be tour guides or art experts. This is your opportunity to tell your partner and all innocent passers-by everything you don't know about art from a professional perspective. Have fun with your partner choosing a gallery where you can go and offer the town's commoners some of your omniscient wisdom. Choose an outfit that will help you play the part, and spend your time moving from artwork to artwork, making enlightened speeches and declarations about each work. If you're lucky, you may even become involved in a conversation with the gallery's curator, and that's when you're going to have to try and educate them as best you can. All in the name of fun. Alternatively, you and your partner can have an absurd intellectual debate about each artwork and then find out who's opinion was closest to the truth. I'd suggest going for a drink afterwards.

Quirky date number seven is kind of romantic in a way. Your *modus operandi* for this date is to build a time capsule. A time capsule is known as a container storing objects representing a specific time, and these objects would represent the present time as it was when they were stored in the container. The container is then buried so it can be discovered by someone in the future. Judging from this definition of a time capsule, it means that you need to choose objects that may carry a specific significance of this time, place them in a container, and bury them in a location that only you two know of. Remember, though, that you shouldn't dig it up later. There are so many different themes and choices of what you can put in your time capsule. Do you want the contents to be a representation of your relationship? Alternatively, do you want to add in a list of the dumbest or cleverest inventions made by humans to give some random aliens a heads-up somewhere in the future? My first choice would be a non-stick frying pan.

On a different note, I wonder if anyone would ever consider putting their wedding day outfits in a time capsule. Imagine digging up a 200-year-old wedding dress! This quirky date idea has the potential to carry a symbolic and romantic reference that will only be known by you and your partner.

Spoiler alert for quirky date number eight: if you're not into online gaming, this idea may not be for you. However, if you are open to new experiences, you may just enjoy this date immensely. The quirky date idea is to play an online MMORPG game, which is a role-playing game where a large number of participants can play at the same time ("MMORPG," 2020). Popular MMORPG games you can try out include World of Warcraft, The Elder Scrolls, or Star Wars: The Old Republic. If you want to go old-school, the most popular MMORPG games you can go for are Asheron's Call or Asheron's Call 2, which were released in the 90s. Other choices include RuneScape from 2001, Guild Wars from 2005, or Lineage, also released in 2005 (Trent, 2016). It's all about new experiences, right? However, for this date, you may need some essential equipment and specific graphics requirements. There may be a gaming facility nearby that can provide you with this equipment, so be sure to try this one out.

Quirky date number nine is all about connecting with the hidden artist in you. For this quirky adventure, you'll need canvasses and paint or charcoal, depending on whether you like drawing or painting. You can use pencils, but artist's charcoal adds a nice smoky look to your art. You are going to paint each other ("200 Date Ideas - The Only List You'll Need to Find the Perfect Date Idea," 2020). This is your chance to be really creative, and you may even conjure up a masterpiece that you can hang in the dining room. There are endless options on how you can approach your artistic process. Would you like to draw or paint each other in the nude or in special outfits? Do you want to conduct some research first and prepare the canvas with a pencil sketch before you start painting, or do you want to go all out abstract expressionist and paint your partner as an orange blob? Who knows, they may be into that. Another really fun technique is to draw with your eyes closed. Take a few moments to look at your partner and then close your eyes while you're drawing or painting on the canvas. You'll be surprised at the characteristics you've instinctually added to your image and how they may resemble your partner's physical appearance. This will, of course, end up as an abstract work, except if you were peeking. This is a beautiful way of showing your partner in a raw and open way how you see them from your artist's eye. Even if you are not an artist, we are all capable of expression and all forms of expression have significance and beauty.

Finally, we've reached quirky date number 10. We saved the naughtiest one for last. For quirky date number 10, you and your partner need to conduct some thorough research and go skinny dipping. The research is paramount because you don't want to get caught and you don't want to get bitten by an alligator. Try to find a scenic location, and you can even consider doing this while going away for the weekend to a place that provides this kind of environment. If you're afraid someone may see you, do a quickie. Plan your timing to make sure you don't give an innocent passer-by a heart attack. If you see one, just smile, wave, and put on that bathing suit with lightning speed. Then, go and enjoy a well-deserved cocktail.

This list includes a date idea for every type and taste, while still being quirky and challenging. The important component of these dates is the element of teamwork and camaraderie that needs to exist between you and your partner as well as your inspiration and willingness to make each date a fun and unique experience. These are the elements that will support true relationship building and develop trust and openness between you as a couple. Go on and try them out and let go of the seriousness for a little while.

Chapter 10:

Don't Forget About Sex

Sex, along with communication and self-care, form the foundation of a healthy relationship. These components are also all interlinked, but sex plays an important role in the healthy functioning of the human body. Sex is not only about reproduction as compared to most animals, but it is also about pleasure and intimacy. Sexual intercourse and masturbation have proven to positively affect the intellectual, physical, psychological, social, and emotional aspects of human life.

Sex also benefits the body physically by being a form of cardiovascular exercise, and study has shown that sex can improve the health of your heart, burn some unwanted calories, lower your blood pressure, make you stronger, and increase your libido. Additionally, people who have active sex lives also tend to be active or exercise regularly, and they tend to have healthier eating habits (Gotter & Rogers, 2018). So, it appears that people with healthy habits have lots of sex and lots of sex can offer health benefits.

Many studies have been conducted on the effects and benefits of sex, and one specific study that was conducted on couples who had sex twice a week as opposed to couples who had sex less frequently showed that frequent sexual activity leads to improved immunity. Researchers came to this conclusion by testing the levels of immunoglobulin A, which is an antibody, in the participants' saliva. The participating couples who had sex more frequently had higher levels of immunoglobulin in their saliva.

Sex also causes the release of oxytocin and endorphins during an orgasm. Oxytocin is known as the "love" and "intimacy" hormone, and the combination of oxytocin and endorphins acts like a sedative, which makes you sleep like a baby. This restful and deep sleep you get from your hormonal sedative leads to more health benefits that include more energy, another contribution towards a healthy immune system, and living longer.

Apart from sex, masturbation also has specific benefits along with similar benefits to sex. Masturbation can help you to understand how your body works. Even if you are married, this doesn't mean that you can't learn from your body by masturbating. It allows your body to reach a point of climax or orgasm more easily and it is also a natural way of treating different forms of sexual dysfunctions. Masturbation can make sex more satisfying for partners and it boosts a person's self-esteem and confidence level. Finally, the likelihood of contracting an STI or HIV is at its lowest when masturbating. On your own, of course.

Finally, there is some other good news that comes with having lots of sex. For example, people who have sex often tend to look younger up to seven to twelve years. An interesting fact linked to these individuals is that they are also comfortable with their sexual identity and expressing their sexuality. Other than that, sex and masturbation help with mental health issues like depression and anxiety and increase your level of happiness and satisfaction in life (Gotter & Rogers, 2018).

The Importance of Healthy Sex

Healthy sex is crucial for a healthy relationship. To have healthy sex is synonymous with a healthy mind and a healthy body, as well as your ability to own your sexual choices and actions. If you are able to accept yourself as a sexual being and you are comfortable with who you are, you make it easier for your partner to connect with you. Apart from the physical benefits of sex, there are also the emotional and psychological payoffs of a secure and healthy sexual relationship. Healthy sex strengthens the bond in a relationship because feeling accepted and desired on such an intimate level builds trust, confidence, and a general sense of wellbeing. The difference between healthy sex in a relationship and unhealthy sex is that unhealthy sex is solely about physical gratification, while healthy sex is about the connection of two souls.

There are a lot of misconceptions about what good sex and healthy sex is supposed to be and supposed to be like. For example, couples feel that it's their responsibility to experience an orgasm every time they have sex. If this is the most important aspect of having sex with your partner, then your goals sway more towards physical gratification. I'm, of course, not saying that never having an orgasm is healthy, but if it doesn't happen every time, it shouldn't be regarded as a sexual weakness or as an indication that your partner doesn't find you sexually attractive. Was the rest of the journey not worth anything, and did you not experience anything special during any other stage while you were being intimate with your partner? Use this time to explore and experience each other instead of pointedly working towards having an orgasm (Rosen, 2018). Understanding these situations and accepting them unconditionally will strengthen your bond and can even improve your sex life.

Another aspect of healthy sex lies in the state of mind both partners are in before they engage in any sort of sexual act. This ties back to the fact that there should always be a mutual understanding of respect between partners and they should be able to express their feelings freely and openly without any fear of negative repercussions. The same applies to sex. If your partner wants to have sex and you don't, they need to respect this decision. The situation may be different if one partner is refusing sex to "punish" the other for some reason, but the situation we are talking about here is when one partner genuinely does not want to have sex for a particular reason. There always needs to be that level of respect and, as we mentioned above, sex should not be used as a tool to manipulate or punish your partner ("Sex and Healthy Relationships," n.d.).

Here's another frequently asked question: how often is healthy? Well, are we all the same or are we all individuals? You may be able to draw a broad estimate by saying if you're married and you haven't had sex in the past five years, there may be a problem. Similarly, you may conclude that if you're married and you and your partner both decided to quit your jobs just so you can have sex all day and all night, that's also not quite normal. I can, with confidence, assume we are all somewhere in between. However, because sex is linked to physical health and a decrease of anxiety, that can be one reason to increase sexual activity in your relationship from a rational perspective. It's interesting how some people want to know what everyone else is doing to such an extent that they stop focusing on their own relationships. "Hey Babe, Betty and Jim from next door had sex three times last night, d'ya think we can beat them?" Poor Babe, whatever their name is. Don't you think telling that to your partner can make them feel like the one hell of an effort they put in just couldn't satisfy you? Healthy sex is not a competition with your friends or neighbors and keeping the details between the two of you keeps it special and exciting.

However, if you are desperate for some statistics, the average number of times couples have sex per week is once. If you want to measure the quality of your sex life against some kind of standard, then I guess a legitimate statistic is better than the antics going on next door. The study that is linked to this statistic provides further valuable and interesting information about couples and how frequently they have sex. The couples who showed an average of one sexual encounter a week were asked to double their sexual activity to twice a week. This request was specifically made to see if increased sexual activity will improve their relationship dynamics and wellbeing. The conclusion is quite surprising. Decreased frequency in sexual activity indicates a lower level of wellbeing, but when sexual activity between couples reaches the frequency of once a week or more, there are few to no changes. A possible explanation for this is that the second weekly sexual encounter in the experiment did not happen spontaneously, which meant that it may not have had the same positive effects. So, having sex once a week seems to not only be the average, but also healthy for most couples (Church, 2019).

Are Men Really from Mars and Women Really From Venus?

It may feel that way sometimes, and if you look at the different ways sex affects the male and female body, it appears to be even more evident. However, from a rational perspective, men and women need to be on the same planet to have sex, and I suspect that if they came from two different planets, a huge fight would break out about which planet is most superior for having sex on. In other words, let's rule out the Venus/Mars possibility altogether.

We can, however, look at how the male and female body respond to sex. First, men get major preventive benefits for prostate cancer. These benefits depend on the frequency of penile-vaginal intercourse and also on how frequently a man ejaculates. A man who ejaculates 4.6 to 7 times a week had a significantly reduced risk of developing prostate cancer before the age of 70, which is a reduction of 36%. There's only one thing I'd like to know, and that's what a 0.6 ejaculation looks like in comparison to a 1.0 ejaculation. I guess every bit helps, so that's probably not so important. Sex can also affect a man's mortality. This was indicated during a ten-year follow up study where men who experienced orgasms twice a week or more lowered their mortality risk by 50% (Gotter & Rogers, 2018).

Women have loads of benefits when it comes to sex. Maybe it's to spur them on a bit to, you know, help the men avoid prostate cancer. An orgasm for a woman not only increases blood flow but it also releases chemicals that act as a natural aid for pain relief. Frequent sex can help women with incontinence, improve bladder control, build strong pelvic muscles, act as a protective measure against conditions like endometriosis, improve fertility, and even help with menstrual cramps and PMS. The only problem is, the last thing a woman probably wants to do while experiencing premenstrual cramps is to have sex. If you are currently going through menopause or have had this experience recently, it's also helpful to note that staying sexually active after menopause prevents vaginal atrophy, which is the thinning of the vaginal wall. Vaginal atrophy can cause urinary issues and painful sex (Gotter & Rogers, 2018). We are never too old to have this intimate and special experience with our partner, and its effects always benefit our bodies.

We've covered the basic differences of the physical, but how do a woman's sexual desires compare to a man's? If you're two females or males in the relationship, how can this information benefit your sexual dynamics? In the past, most sexologists and sex experts were male, so the theory behind desire, whether it be for males or females, were from a male perspective. The input from female sex therapists and sexologists changed how female sexual desire and its nature was understood, and it has illuminated the theory about the way women think about sex. The most basic component of women that most of us are aware of is that women are naturally emotive and emotionally instinctive. So, it is no surprise that this also plays a role when it comes to sexual desire. For women, sex can be and is a physical desire, but when in an intimate relationship, there is more often than not a deeper reason forming the foundation for their sexual desire. This means that women don't see pure carnal lust as a good enough reason to have sex, especially if they are in a meaningful relationship like a marriage. They want the sexual encounter to have meaning, so there needs to be a reason behind it (Snyder, 2020). This instinctive reasoning behind a woman's sexual desires is also required for bonding to take place during sex and for the sexual experience to have meaning and relevance between two loving partners. Instead of a carnal type of arousal, a woman prefers an authentic arousal that is unique to her and her relationship with her partner. This can make a man seem animalistic and primal, but they actually just even out the balance and complete the puzzle. Let's look at some typical differences in how males and females view sex.

In terms of orientation, science admits that men are the physical ones. Women, contrastingly, tend to be more relational. This is why physical oneness is important to men while emotional oneness is important to women in terms of sex. Priority-wise, sex is way at the top for men, while women may have other more important priorities, which may point to the evolutionary footprint of motherhood.

Stimulating a man is easier than stimulating a woman, if you know where to touch him. However, men are also turned on by smell and are well-known for being visual creatures. Women are also turned on by touch, but not the same kind as men. I daresay you're not going to turn a woman on with such a direct approach. Women are also sensitive to a partner's attitude, words, and actions, which means you really need to be immersed in the moment and be focused on her to turn her on.

When it comes to physical sexual responses and orgasms, the Mars and Venus theory comes to mind again; but hey, we've debunked it, haven't we? For example, a man's sexual responses are quick, he is an instinctive initiator, and once he's into it, nothing's going to distract him. Women, on the other hand, are the complete opposite according to science. They experience a slow development of excitement, they instinctually tend to be the responder rather than the initiator, and they are easily distracted, even during sex. A man's orgasm is also physically-oriented, which largely consists of a physical sensation, while a woman's experience has a significant emotional component. A man requires an orgasm or ejaculation for satisfaction, while a woman doesn't need an orgasm to feel sexually satisfied. This is also because of the difference between the physical male orientation and the emotional female orientation (Rainey, D. & Rainey, B., 2012).

These are characteristics that have been observed in male and female behavior. However, is this information accurate in every case, and is every person a typical male and female? Take your partner, for example. How do these factoids compare to the characteristics and habits of your partner? It's easier for science to categorize and compartmentalize, but when it comes to sexuality, which has also been argued to be more of a spectrum or a sliding scale, you will also find individuals who have both "male" and "female" characteristics. It depends on where you identify or stand on the spectrum.

Sexy Strategies

If you've skipped the whole book just to read this section first, you won't be disappointed. Sometimes couples need a few fresh strategies just to reignite their sex life. Does it feel like you've been married for centuries? Well, you need to snap out of it and become naughty again! Relearn how to make your partner want you. Because your partner does want you; you just need to iron out the nitty-gritty communication issues. Here are your go-to sexy strategies to get that flame going again.

The first strategy you can try is some Saucy Sexting. Start your quest by calling your partner to the bedroom and asking them to lie down next to you. Make sure they have their phone with them, and if they don't, just say that you'll be right back, go and fetch the phone, and casually place it on their bedside table. Then, just start sexting them. After you've started your sexting liaison, don't talk or look at them, even if they try to talk to you. Let them get the message that you are only available via text, and most importantly, only via sext. Watch how your idea slowly starts to germinate in their mind like a tiny sex seed and become a budding little plant of lust. Nurture and cultivate that little plant by telling your partner all kinds of things that make them incredibly turned on, but don't allow them to touch you. How long you want to keep this going is up to you. The longer the better, but don't let it fizzle out. Wait until your sex plant is in full bloom, which will be when your partner is clutching the bed due to clearly wanting to tear off your clothes. You can even remove one piece of clothing at a time during your sexting session until you are only wearing one strategic piece. But remember, no touching until you say so! Use this as a foreplay strategy. Prepare yourself for some explosive sex.

The next strategy may upset some viewers. This strategy includes taking the TV out of the bedroom! Nobody's going to have any sex ever if your evening routine is falling asleep every night while watching a crime drama. I know, people are very attached to their TV's, and this may cause conflict. If your partner doesn't want to budge, then you may need to come to an agreement about dedicating certain nights to each other and to being intimate. You can even use the TV if you are into watching erotic films. However, take time to shut off the TV and spend time together intimately. Leave your partner a reminder on their phone that tonight is No-TV night and tell them what you have in mind for the evening. In other words, let them look forward to those nights when you're not allowed to switch on the TV.

Reading to each other sounds boring, but it depends on what you are reading. Think along the lines of erotic literature and saucy blogs. Take turns to read sexually charged literature to each other, either while one of you is blindfolded or by looking each other straight in the eye. The point here is for your partner to hear you voicing these erotic ideas and vice versa because voicing it brings it one step closer to becoming a reality. So, when it's your turn to read, don't be shy. You can even turn it into a role-playing situation. Articulate sexually charged words and read the literature as if doing what the characters are doing is your greatest desire and you want to do the same to your partner. Experience the words you are reading vividly and notice the impact your performance is making on your partner. You start out fully clothed, naked, or in your underwear, and incorporate a process of slowly undressing each other. You'll both know when it's time to toss the book aside.

The final sexy strategy is to leave your foreplay up to lady luck. You can either purchase a sexy game set that contains dice with all sorts of naughty instructions on it, or you can both take pieces of paper and pens, write down things you've always wanted your partner to do to you, and throw them in two separate containers. You have to make at least five each. You can prepare the area beforehand or you can do this as a spontaneous game. Make sure that there's something special to drink and eat that your partner enjoys. Now you just need to take turns in drawing those ideas or roll the dice. Set up some game rules beforehand if you are using your own game. For example, you have to complete a certain number of cards to complete the game. Clothed or in the buff? Absolutely up to you. Enjoy!

To make these strategies work in your favor, you need to be the poster-person of confidence, sensuality, and enthusiasm. Use what you know about your partner to your advantage to lure them into the games. Especially if you plan to use these games to improve sex between you and your partner, that requires some resurrective assistance. Be playful and tease your partner in the ways and places that turn them on. If your partner doesn't bite the first time, don't be discouraged.

Read This if You Play with Toys

Toys are not everyone's cup of tea, but they can definitely spice up your sex life, enable your ability to or intensify your orgasms, help you to experience multiple orgasms, and turn sex into a fun game whether it's only the two of you or if you're into group sessions. All of the toys I'll be describing below are available on online stores like Amazon, so you can track them down by just entering the name of any toy in the platform's search box. Let's explore the best and most highly rated sex toys from the pleasure industry.

Our first super-stimulator is called the "Partner Whale." This is because it kind of looks like a blue whale that has its mouth wide open. The upper part is wider and should be placed on the clitoris, while the lower part should be inserted into the vagina. Both sides vibrate, so while your clitoris is being stimulated during sex, your partner is getting the ultimate massage while your g-spot is also getting a tickle. After positioning and inserting the wondrous whale into yourself, your partner can enter you for a multi-functional and explosive orgasmic experience.

The Ohare Double Vibrating Rabbit Cock Ring is about as kinky as it sounds. With a double ring, bullet, and two perky rabbit ears, its mission is to take you and your partner to Climax Ville together. This double-duty sex wonder is built to stimulate a simultaneous orgasm between partners as the rabbit ears stimulate your clitoris while the vibrating cock ring is happily buzzing away against his shaft. If you're looking for that step up to experiencing simultaneous orgasms for the first time or more regularly, this little black bunny ring may be your best option.

If you want to wear your toy all day just in case you feel like climaxing in the office restroom, the We-Vibe Moxie is a great option. It's cute and small and fits right in your underwear using a magnetic clip. This nifty toy is so quiet that no-one will ever suspect anything—from the toy, that is. You and your partner can download the app, and your partner can decide to surprise you with some office foreplay even if they're on the other side of town.

The Flamingo is a great choice for same-sex couples who are looking for some serious clitoral stimulation. This puppy is app-controlled and has nine different vibration modes, and like the Partner Whale, it does a simultaneous g-spot and clitoral stimulation. The difference here is that the bottom part that inserts into the vagina is bigger for more penetrative stimulation. You can use it on your own or use it to pleasure your partner. In true flamingo style, it comes in a bright fuschia that will likely match the color of your cheeks after using it.

The Lelo Ida looks like a technologically advanced sex toy that should render technologically advanced results. Apparently, it does. It provides simultaneous stimulation for the clitoris and penis by working as a cock ring but that is worn by the female partner. It comes with a matching remote that fits in the palm of your hand, so you can up or down your pleasure levels with only a little squeeze and a moan. Both the toy and the remote come in a bright pink with a stylish metallic finish.

Our next toy is definitely one of a kind. This is also the most diverse toy that can be used for vaginal penetration, anal penetration, and clitoral stimulation. It's called the Complete Le Wand Pleasure Set, and the package comes with a sassy vibrating wand in white and several darkish-grey, silicone-ish wand covers that are all differently textured. There are two different clitoral stimulators and three covers for the tip of the wand that sport strategically placed knobs, grooves, and little bumps. You are bound to hit several jackpots with this one because of its versatility, and the Le Wand is specifically made for clitoral stimulation, g-spot stimulation, and vaginal and anal pleasuring. Grab the lube!

If there's two vaginas involved, then this accessory may come in handy. The Tomboi Harness looks like normal underwear, but it provides sturdy support for a dildo. Any dildo, according to its description. I suggest you test this one out using the Double Dildo, which is also made for couples with two vaginas. The one side is egg-shaped, while the other side resembles two very long and curved fingers. Sleek and black in color, this toy may reach depths you never thought possible (Gainsburg et al., 2020).

Conclusion

It's difficult to stick to one tone when writing about marriage and relationships. That is because relationships themselves are so multi-faceted and they can be fickle in nature, even if it's a stable relationship. Because of what we know about intimate relationships, it is so important to understand and build on the important foundations of relationships and marriage. These foundations include communication, self-care, and healthy sex. The information in this book can provide advice and suggestions on how to tackle different issues and what the best way is to communicate, for example, but each individual still has their own unique way of doing things and each relationship has authentic traits. Remember the chipped plate and be proud of it. Also keep in mind that if the chip has become a crack that may weaken the plate, then it needs to be fixed. If you are in a relationship with someone, communication methods and strategies can be adapted to best fit you and the person you love and who you want to spend the rest of your life with. It actually starts with knowing and understanding yourself. If you married someone and you didn't know or understand yourself at that point, it is never too late to start this journey, and by being open with your partner, you can develop your own authentic method of open and loving communication.

When it comes to communication, remember to put yourself in your partner's shoes and to practice deep and active listening. These methods will help your partner to open up and be honest with you if they can see that you are attentive and that what they have to say is important to you. There will be moments of conflict, but if these moments are steered in the right direction, they can lead to relationship growth and considerable improvement in the health of your relationship or marriage. Don't fight each other, tackle the issue. Also aim to incorporate a proactive attitude in not only your relationship, but also your life in general. Don't let small things upset you or affect your relationship and be an inspiration to your partner. It is especially hard if your partner suffers from an illness or chronic condition. You can help them by loving and listening unconditionally and by reassuring them that they can lean on you for support.

The point of meeting your forever mate is to grow old with them and to be with them 'til death to you part. You can be a formidable team by making sure that you are not only in a solid partnership and act as a unit, but that both partners can also function as individuals. As you make time for each other, so should you also make time for yourself and do what you love. Try not to resent your partner if they need space or if they are not able to tell you about their problems immediately. Patience builds trust and mutual acceptance, which are two of the most beautiful signs of a blooming marriage. Look after yourself mentally and physically, as this will show that you are proud to be you and to be in the partnership that you're in. Your partner chose you for a reason, and that reason is because you are your authentic self. We are all beautiful as individuals, and we should embrace our individuality and diversity instead of agonizing over that which makes us different. Do all the things that make you feel fulfilled and never lose your sense of style!

Be sexy. Be sexual. We all are unique in our own way. True sexiness is not about looking at what other couples are doing but doing your own thing and what gives you and your partner the most pleasure. Communication also plays a role in having a healthy sexual relationship because both partners need to be open about what pleases them and what turns them off. If you need to reignite the flame, take an approach that you know will turn your partner on. Surprise them, spoil them, and tease them. Sex is healthy for the mind and body.

Finally, if you're into toys, I'm sure you saw one that will rock your boat. I saw one too, but I'm keeping it a secret! Keep yours a secret as well, and only tell your partner. You can even surprise them by whipping it out one night. If it's just between you two, it's exciting and special, just like you are. If you're getting that one you can clip onto your panties and wear to work, just try not to be too loud.

References

200 date ideas - The only list you'll need to find the perfect date idea (2020). Conversation Starters World. https://conversationstartersworld.com/date-ideas/

Admin. (2020, April 6). How to overcome insecurity in a relationship. Real Life Counselling. https://www.reallifecounselling.com/2020/04/2020-03-how-to-overcome-insecurity-in-a-relationship/

Andrews, T. (2020, November 19). K, you've heard of love languages, but let's discuss apology languages. Cosmopolitan. https://www.cosmopolitan.com/sex-love/a34731670/apology-language/

Are your hormones ruining your relationship? (2018, October 18). DWC. https://www.dailywellness.com/2018/10/18/hormones-ruining-your-relationship/

Benniger, M. (2020, November 11). Know your love language: Learn to speak "physical touch". Www.Blinkist.com. https://www.blinkist.com/magazine/posts/love-language-physical-touch

Benninger, M. (2019, November 19). Know your love language: Learn to speak "quality time" - Blinkist Magazine. @blinkist; Blinkist. https://www.blinkist.com/magazine/posts/love-language-quality-time

Beohm, R. (2018, June 27). What to do when you see "negative" body language. Rachel Beohm: Writer, Speaker, Coach. https://www.rachelbeohm.com/what-to-do-when-you-see-negative-body-language/

Brandt, A. (2018, October 1). How reactive behavior damages your relationships. Psychology Today. https://www.psychologytoday.com/za/blog/mindful-anger/201810/how-reactive-behavior-damages-your-relationships

Church, C. (2019). Will having more sex improve your relationship? Smart Couples. https://smartcouples.ifas.ufl.edu/married/sex-and-intimacy/will-having-more-sex-improve-your-relationship/

Collins, S., & Collins, O. (2020, August 8). 10 sneaky effects of jealousy on you and your relationship. YourTango. https://www.yourtango.com/experts/susie-and-otto-collins/10-things-you-dont-know-about-jealousy-you-should

Desanctis, E. (2019, January 25). What "I'm sorry" means when it's used to manipulate you. One Love Foundation. https://www.joinonelove.org/learn/what-im-sorry-means-when-its-used-to-manipulate-you/

Dodgson, L. (2018, October 24). 11 signs your old relationships are affecting your current one. Business Insider. https://www.businessinsider.com/signs-your-old-relationships-are-affecting-your-current-one-2018-6

Dolan, E. W. (2020, February 15). Study: Women evaluate partners more negatively when estrogen is elevated—And men know it. PsyPost. https://www.psypost.org/2020/02/study-women-evaluate-partners-more-negatively-when-estrogen-is-elevated-and-men-know-it-55704#:~:text=Social%20Psychology-

Fashion as a self-care tool. (2020). Connected Apparel. https://connectedapparel.com/blogs/news/self-care-healthier-you-fashion-self-care

Fetters, A. K. (2014, June 3). 11 ways to childproof your relationship before getting pregnant. Explore Parents. https://www.parents.com/pregnancy/considering-baby/is-it-time/save-relationship-before-getting-pregnant/

Gainsburg, M., Rimm, H., Bacharach, E., & Engle, G. (2020, August 29). 24 best sex toys for couples in 2020. Women's Health. https://www.womenshealthmag.com/sex-and-love/g19984127/best-couples-sex-toys/

Gersho, B. (n.d.). How voice tone affects your relationships: "It's not what you say…" . The Relationship Doc. https://www.therelationshipdoc.org/how-voice-tone-affects-your-relationships-its-not-what-you-say/

Gordon, E. V. (2019, November 22). Two things you don't need to know about your partner—& 6 things you do. Www.Refinery29.Com. https://www.refinery29.com/en-us/sharing-relationship-history-advice

Gotter, A. & Rogers, P. (2018, October 18). The health benefits of sex. Healthline. https://www.healthline.com/health/healthy-sex-health-benefits

Gould, W. R., & Blackburn, S. (2020, July 1). What the receiving gifts love language means for a relationship. Verywell Mind. https://www.verywellmind.com/receiving-gifts-love-language-4783665

Greenwald, M. (2019, November 3). 30 body language cues that indicate relationship trouble. Best Life. https://bestlifeonline.com/relationship-body-language-cues/

Gunther, R. (2020, January 31). How self-centered pride destroys intimacy. Psychology Today. https://www.psychologytoday.com/us/blog/rediscovering-love/202001/how-self-centered-pride-destroys-intimacy

Gurevich, R. (2020, March 6). How to have a baby and building your family when you identify as LGBTQ. Verywell Family. https://www.verywellfamily.com/what-are-gay-couples-options-for-having-babies-4172970#:~:text=Insemination%20with%20a%20sperm%20donor

Holl, T. (2018, December 14). 8 date ideas that double as self-care, because you both deserve to treat yo selves. Elite Daily.

https://www.elitedaily.com/p/8-date-ideas-that-double-as-self-care-because-you-both-deserve-to-treat-yo-selves-15521423

Howard, L. (2018, March 7). 7 things you don't need to apologize for in a relationship. Bustle. https://www.bustle.com/p/7-things-you-dont-need-to-apologize-for-in-a-relationship-8416034

Koenig, R. (2019, March 15). 10 parent date night ideas you'll actually want to do. SheKnows. https://www.sheknows.com/parenting/articles/2017297/parent-date-night-ideas/

Magee, E. (2019, March 1). 7 ways couples can practice self-care together. Mindbodygreen. https://www.mindbodygreen.com/articles/couples-practice-self-care-together

Menasce Horowitz, J., Graf, N., & Livingston, G. (2019, November 6). Marriage and cohabitation in the U.S. Pew Research Center's Social & Demographic Trends Project. https://www.pewsocialtrends.org/2019/11/06/marriage-and-cohabitation-in-the-u-s/

MMORPG. (2020). Dictionary.com. https://www.dictionary.com/browse/mmorpg?s=t

Moody, LaCroix Design Co. (2019). 5 Love Languages - The 5 Love Languages®. The 5 Love Languages®. https://www.5lovelanguages.com/5-love-languages/

Nguyen, J. (2020, August 14). What it really means to have "Acts of Service" as your Love Language. Mindbodygreen. https://www.mindbodygreen.com/articles/acts-of-service-love-language

Nguyen, J., & Jacobs Hendel, H. (2020, May 25). What it really means to have words of affirmation as a Love Language. Mindbodygreen. https://www.mindbodygreen.com/articles/how-to-use-words-of-affirmation#:~:text=Words%20of%20affirmation%20are%20any

Powell, R. (2016, October 22). 9 things I wish I'd known before I adopted a child. The Guardian. https://www.theguardian.com/lifeandstyle/2016/oct/22/9-things-i-wish-id-known-before-i-adopted-a-child

PsychAlive. (2010, March 26). How jealousy destroys relationships. https://www.psychalive.org/how-jealousy-destroys-relationships/#:~:text=One%20of%20the%20most%20harmful

PsychAlive. (2015, January 23). How to overcome insecurity: Why am I so insecure? https://www.psychalive.org/how-to-overcome-insecurity/

Raab, D. (2017, August 9). Deep listening in personal relationships. Psychology Today. https://www.psychologytoday.com/za/blog/the-empowerment-diary/201708/deep-listening-in-personal-relationships

Rainey, D., & Rainey, B. (2012, March 26). How do men and women differ in how they view sex? FamilyLife. https://www.familylife.com/articles/topics/marriage/marriage-challenges/understanding-differences/how-do-men-and-women-differ-in-how-they-view-sex/

Roberts, E. (2015, September 12). Why self-care is important for your physical and mental health. Healthyplace.Com. https://www.healthyplace.com/blogs/buildingselfesteem/2015/09/why-self-care-is-important-for-your-mental-physical-health

Rosen, P. (2018, April 6). Healthy sex: The ultimate guide. EverydayHealth.Com. https://www.everydayhealth.com/healthy-sex/

Santos-Longhurst, A., & Pelley, V. (2018, August 30). Why is oxytocin known as the 'love hormone'? And 11 other FAQs. Healthline. https://www.healthline.com/health/love-hormone

Scott, E., & Goldman, R. (2020, April 18). The importance of apologizing for relationship repair. Verywell Mind. https://www.verywellmind.com/the-importance-of-apologizing-

3144986#:~:text=Apologizing%20helps%20repair%20relationships%2
0by

Seetubtim, M. (2014, October 14). 7 important lessons you can only
learn from a failed relationship. Thought Catalog.
https://thoughtcatalog.com/mo-seetubtim/2014/10/7-important-
lessons-you-can-only-learn-from-a-failed-relationship/

Segal, J., Smith, M., Robinson, L., & Boose, G. (2019). Nonverbal
communication. HelpGuide.Org.
https://www.helpguide.org/articles/relationships-
communication/nonverbal-communication.htm

Sex and healthy relationships. (n.d.). Loveisrespect.Org.
https://www.loveisrespect.org/healthy-relationships/sex-and-healthy-
relationships/#:~:text=Healthy%20Sex%20is%20About%20Respect

Sinrich, J. (2018, September 24). The best age to get pregnant,
according to moms. Explore Parents.
https://www.parents.com/getting-pregnant/age/timing/the-best-age-
to-get-pregnant-according-to-moms/

Sinrich, J. (2019, February 15). Experts say these six body language
signs speak to the strength of your relationship. Martha Stewart.
https://www.marthastewart.com/7883247/body-language-signs-
strong-relationship

Snyder, S. (2020). Women's sexual desire, and why men often don't
recognize it. Sexualityresource.Com.
https://www.sexualityresource.com/blog/womens-sexual-desire-and-
why-men-often-dont-recognize-it

Steber, C. (2017, August 18). These are the 11 things most likely to end
your long-term relationship, according to research. Bustle.
https://www.bustle.com/p/these-are-the-11-things-most-likely-to-
end-your-long-term-relationship-according-to-research-76805

Steber, C. (2018, August 16). 7 things from the past you should tell
your partner about vs. 3 you shouldn't. Bustle.

https://www.bustle.com/p/7-things-from-the-past-you-should-tell-your-partner-about-vs-3-you-shouldnt-10083578

The top 13 meditation tips. (2020). Headspace. https://www.headspace.com/meditation/tips

Trent, R. (2016, January 6). 20 old MMORPGs that you can still play. Www.Mmogames.Com. https://www.mmogames.com/gamearticles/20-old-mmorpgs-can-still-play/

What does your tone of voice convey? (2018, June 18). Exploring Your Mind. https://exploringyourmind.com/what-does-your-tone-of-voice-convey/

Young, K. (2015, March 2). Fighting fair in a relationship: How to get what you need and stay close while you do it. Hey Sigmund. https://www.heysigmund.com/fighting-fair/

www.ingramcontent.com/pod-product-compliance
Lightning Source LLC
Chambersburg PA
CBHW060052100426
42742CB00014B/2796